Brexit: What the Hell Happens Now?
Praise for the first edition

...ng for a good guide to Brexit and what comes next,
...nd Ian Dunt's *What the Hell Happens Now?*

— Tom Watson, Deputy Leader, Labour Party

... easily digestible. I'd encourage anyone who is confused,
... rustrated by Brexit to read this book – you'll be far wiser by

— Caroline Lucas, Co-Leader, Green Party

... and necessarily brutal... Whatever your position during the
... you ought to read Dunt because he is willing to face uncom-
... Highly recommended.

— Nick Cohen, *The Spectator*

...angers who weep for the days when Britannia ruled the waves
...her with this book. Nor will it be of interest to [left] fantasists.
...se could learn a great deal.

— James Coldwell, *Fabian Review*

...y recommend Ian Dunt's excellent guide. Dunt has taken
... step of asking a set of experts what they think. I learnt a
... en happens when I have the humility to listen to experts.

— Philip Collins, *Prospect*

... account of just how much confusion and ignorance has
... this entire debate

— James O'Brien, LBC

First published by Canbury Press, 2016
Reprinted 2016
This edition published in October 2017

Canbury Press,
Kingston upon Thames,
Surrey
www.canburypress.com

Cover: Jade Design

Printed and bound in Great Britain by Clays Ltd, St Ives Plc

FSC

ISBN: 978-0-9954978-5-6 (Paperback)
978-0-9954978-3-2 (Ebook)

BREXIT
What the Hell Happens Now?

Ian Dunt

Canbury PRESS

'I think the people in this country have had enough of experts from organisations with acronyms, saying they know what's best and getting it consistently wrong.'

— Michael Gove,
Brexit campaigner,
Sky News, 3 June 2016*

*When told that the leaders of the US, China, India, the Bank of England, the IMF, the IFS, the CBI, five former NATO secretary generals, the chief executive of the NHS and most trade unions opposed Brexit.

For Tio Amir
Who always took a proper look at things

CONTENTS

INTRODUCTION

30 March 2019

The clock strikes midnight and Britain is out of the European Union. The talks have fallen apart in mutual acrimony. The UK has not secured continued membership of the single market. It doesn't even have access. It is out of the customs union, too. It has no trade deals with Europe or anyone else. It is on its own.

In the early morning, a lorry is loaded in Glasgow with radio equipment bound for the Czech Republic. When the lorry arrives at Calais, it is stopped by a customs official. Until today, Britain has enjoyed a seamless trading relationship with Europe. It means that European Union countries recognise UK standards and paperwork and vice-versa, allowing goods to be transported over borders without additional checks. Now the paperwork is worthless. Everything has to be checked.

The lorry is stopped and detained. Inspectors come on board and take samples to send off for testing. Everything will have to be assessed, from the information on the packaging to the environmental impact of the components. This will take several days, during which the lorry is barred from entering the European market.

Behind the Glasgow lorry, several other vehicles are taken to one side. By sunset, the bottleneck on the French side means that lorries can no longer drive onto Calais-bound ferries at Dover. They queue on the slow lane of the A2. Within a few days, the tailback stretches back to London.

For exporters of animal products such as meat and eggs the problems are more severe still. They are only allowed into the EU through specially designated entry inspection posts, but it has been so long since the UK needed them for trade with Europe that none exist. British exports of salmon, beef, and lamb collapse overnight. In Westminster, ministers demand the immediate creation of the inspection posts, but they have limited leverage with their European partners. A key export industry starts to rot.

The problems aren't restricted to goods heading to the Continent. The EU has mutual recognition agreements with Australia, Canada, China, Israel, Japan, New Zealand and the United States, mimicking the bureaucracy-free trade on the Continent. British goods for the US had been verified by virtue of their EU accreditation. Now they also need to be checked. Shipments heading for America's west coast are stopped at customs, detained and sent off for inspection.

In the complex world of freight, with one shipment arriving as the other leaves, the effect is devastating. Brexit detonates like a bomb across global trading networks.

Thousands of large businesses start haemorrhaging cash, but the effect is not limited to goods going out – it hits those coming in, too. Laptop computers from China and Japan are stopped, alongside jeans from the US, French cheese and wine and chocolates from Belgium. Gaps start to appear on shop shelves.

Other bureaucratic requirements re-emerge from the past like zombies. One of them is proof of 'country of origin'. Britain had previously been in the European customs union, which sets tariffs for non-member countries. Imports into the customs union must undergo laborious checks to ensure that they are paying the right tariffs. Each stage in a global manufacturing process must be accounted for; British firms need to present paperwork detailing the origin of every component in their products.

Her Majesty's Revenue and Customs hires an army of inspectors to speed up the process, but they are trying to learn on the go. Many products don't receive their papers in time and don't make it to the border. They sit in the stockroom. In the first year alone, the country of origin requirement costs Britain £25 billion. By 2030 it has reduced GDP by 4.5%.

Products which do make it past border control have tariffs slapped on them. For decades they had been traded freely on the Continent, but those days are over. Cars heading from Britain to Europe – almost half the vehicles made in the UK – are hit by a 10% tariff. Electronic goods are badly affected, as are warships and commercial liners.

Britain's aerospace industry, the second largest in the world, is damaged. The rates of the tariff themselves are fairly modest, hovering between 2.7% and 7.7%, but they don't only go on the finished product when it is sent to Europe. They are also applied to the components shipped from Europe to the UK to make the product. Shares in BAE Systems, Rolls Royce and Airbus plummet. These businesses' costs have rocketed, and their product has shot up in price, without any of the additional revenue flowing to them.

Multiple parts of the British economy, from space stations to cakes, suffer a sudden hit. Companies that still make tangible physical products in Britain – Unilever, Imperial and Penguin among them – are the first to feel the pain.

The big banks in the City of London had been dreading this day. They did what they could to prepare, sacking thousands of middle and low income workers and moving their jobs to EU states. They are desperate to maintain their 'passports', a legal mechanism which allows them to sell financial products across Europe, but to do so they must prove to European regulators that they have a significant presence on the Continent. So they take the cheaper, back-office admin roles and move them, along with one or two executives. Anything else would be a waste of a crisis. This way the banks can kill two birds with one stone: minimising salary costs by transferring the jobs to countries with lower incomes and reducing the damage done by Brexit.

If they are lucky, firms transferred enough functions in time for the March deadline. But others got caught up in another bottleneck – this time of financial authorities. The sleepy, under-staffed regulators in Paris, Warsaw, Frankfurt and Luxembourg couldn't handle the demand for recognition from City firms. Many companies cannot now sell financial products to customers on the mainland. They lose tens of millions of pounds of sales as customers drift off to competitors.

The transfers cut the capacity of London's financial services sector by 10%. Within a year, the City has lost 100,000 jobs and £12 billion in revenue. The pound plunges again. Foreign direct investment falls further. The deficit begins to look unsustainable.

Ironically, immigration starts to decline. Not just from Europe, where immigration controls have been introduced, but from across the world. The economy is tanking and Britain is no longer a country of opportunity.

Years pass, but 2019 comes to be seen as the start of a significant downsizing in the power of the City. Financial services don't have a heart attack. They bleed out.

European regulators start making increased demands on the investment banks with branches in their cities. It starts with requests for more staff but soon includes additional requirements on risk management and capital investment. Firms have to divert more resources to the Continent, but gradually a political dimension develops too. If Europe is where the regulatory decisions are made, perhaps that is where they need to focus their efforts. What began as a technical requirement starts to change into a general financial migration. More and more functions are transferred to the Continent. Less and less money flows into the UK Treasury.

Nissan's car plant in Sunderland is able to survive because of a side deal with the government, in which it was offered relief for any losses caused by Brexit. An offer is also made to BMW. The symbolic effect of Minis with Union Jack roofs being produced in the Czech Republic would have been too much for ministers to bear. Jaguar Land Rover considers the location of its assembly plants in Birmingham, Halewood and Solihull and its three research and development facilities around Warwick. It's not so much the 10% increase in the price of cars, but future regulation that is the worry. Cars are changing. Driverless technology is turning what used to be a lump of metal around some tech into a tech product with a metal shell.

Regulations established now will be with producers for years and they are being made in Brussels, not London. Jaguar Land Rover needs to be whispering into the right person's ear, but British ministers no longer have a seat at the table.

Other less prominent industries warn that they are about to go into a tailspin. Aerospace firms producing commercial and fighter planes in places like Yeovil, Bristol, Stevenage and Portsmouth start laying off workers.

UK negotiators head to the World Trade Organisation (WTO) where Brexit campaigners have long insisted they can fall back onto standard-issue trading rules. But there are no rules governing what Britain has done. They go into a meeting with WTO legal advisers who are divided on how Britain should proceed.

The UK has been trading under an EU umbrella for decades. Now it tries to extract its tariff and subsidy arrangements from the EU and lay them before the rest of the WTO. This triggers an avalanche of legal disputes. WTO rules allow any country that feels it has been unfairly treated to trigger a dispute. Suddenly Britain's fall-back insurance policy looks like a nightmare scenario, with 163 countries able to raise disputes against it on any aspect of its trading arrangements. Some disputes are legitimate. Others, like that made by Argentina, appear to be a way to leverage British vulnerability to regain control of the Falklands. Russia watches from the sidelines, calculating how it might benefit.

Britain argues that it is still party to an EU arrangement preventing the sale of cheap Chinese steel in Europe. Once those floodgates open, the UK knows domestic steel will be unable to compete. China reacts furiously, demanding that

Britain demonstrate domestic injury and unfair trade. But the UK doesn't have an investigating authority capable of undertaking trade remedy investigations. It cannot fight back because it doesn't have the regulatory infrastructure. Steelworkers fear for their livelihoods more than ever before.

The WTO disputes mount up, all demanding high degrees of technical expertise and negotiating experience. British teams do their best, but they are beset by problems from every angle.

In European cities across the Continent, British professionals find they are unable to practise because their qualifications are no longer recognised. Architects, veterinarians, lawyers, medical professionals and countless others realise they have to shut down their company and return to the UK.

No deal has been put in place for legal rulings, so countries across Europe stop recognising court decisions on divorce and child maintenance and other issues made in London. Unseen and mostly unreported, hundreds of single mothers in the UK go without payments from their former partners. A British man who divorced his wife and married again in Italy suddenly finds that the papers are no longer recognised. He is in a state of marital limbo. A hefty chunk of the work done by London's once-thriving lawyers vanishes.

Regulation fails. Britain did not have time to set up all the authorities required to manage industries ranging from patents to medicine. Pharmaceutical firms are thrown into chaos. British regulators are unable to take on the full workload of the European Medicines Agency, so cannot authorise the sale of anti-inflammatory pills, eczema lotions and other treatments to UK patients. British pharmaceutical development slumps into a state of regulatory bafflement.

Regulations across society are in flux. Emergency provisions are made for Single European Sky — which ensures jets fly safely and efficiently — to maintain regulatory authority over UK airspace. But other areas fall into disrepair, causing uncertainty across production lines to complement the chaos in the trading networks.

Against this backdrop, Britain seeks trade deals with its closest allies: Australia and the US. Both countries are wary of talking to the UK without knowing its final status with Europe or the WTO, but there are initial negotiations.

Ahead of talks, the UK prime minister and the US president hold a joint press conference. Downing Street says it shows countries are still keen to trade with the UK, while Washington confirms the US commitment to the special relationship. Then the doors of the negotiating room close and the two leaders are replaced by grim-faced trade experts.

Britain had a chronic shortage of negotiators during the EU talks and the situation has not improved. The ones facing the American team are those who are not required to fight the fires at the WTO. Many are civil servants who have had to read up on trade in the years since Brexit. They face highly specialised trade experts who have been doing this their entire careers.

The public rhetoric disappears. It is replaced by hard-headed demands. US trade officials inform their British counterparts of the reality of the situation. The UK is in a position of unique and historic vulnerability. Investor confidence has dissolved. Its economy is facing its most significant shock since the Second World War. It has no time. It has no negotiating capacity. But Washington wants to help. It is prepared to rush a trade deal through Congress. It could take less than two years. But for this to be achievable, the UK needs to accept all of its demands. The Americans slide a piece of paper across the desk. The British team read the demands: they are horrendous. Consumer protections are reduced across the board, along with environmental regulations and safeguards for the NHS.

UK civil servants have little option but to capitulate. The only way to protect what remains of the British economy is to sell off British sovereignty. The control wrestled from Brussels is now sold off to the highest bidder, behind closed doors, in a conference room in Washington.

What was that?

That was the worst case scenario. It is also Britain's current destination.

It does not need to happen, even now. These are not the consequences of Brexit itself. They are the consequences of a chaotic, hard Brexit. They are what happens when there is insufficient planning, insufficient thinking and a preference for emotion over reason.

Britain can prevent this from happening. All it requires is an intelligent ministerial team, a workable timetable, hundreds of trade experts, a restrained political debate and economic calm.

Britain currently has none of these things.

How did we get here? How did one of the world's most sophisticated political and economic powers find itself driving towards a cliff edge? How did the UK become so lost in rhetoric that this scenario would even be conceivable?

At the core of Britain's current dilemma is a refusal to engage with objective fact. The debate about Brexit was lost, almost as soon as it began, in a tribal and emotional dogfight which bore little relation to reality. That approach continued when the Conservative Party fell apart after the vote and was reassembled by Theresa May.

The British political class does not seem to understand the obstacles that must be overcome, or the profound consequences of failure. They have misunderstood the EU, misunderstood Article 50, misunderstood the WTO, misunderstood the economy and misunderstood the legal framework in which they must now operate.

This book is an attempt to address that. Based on extensive research and discussions with leading experts in politics, the law, markets and Europe, it maps the road ahead, with its multiple hazards and dangers.

The first step towards preventing a catastrophe is understanding that one is looming.

What did we vote for?

The starting point for our current difficulties lies in the referendum question itself.

On 23 June 2016, voters in the UK were asked: 'Should the United Kingdom remain a member of the European Union or leave the European Union.' The results were:

Remain **16,141,241 (48.1%)**
Leave **17,410,742 (51.9%)**

One million more people voted out. Unless there is a sudden and unexpected change in the political weather, Britain is leaving. But there are many different ways to leave the EU.

You don't have to be in the European Union to be part of the customs union mentioned in the last chapter. Nor do you have to be in the European Union to be in the single market.

The single market is the big trading arrangement that allows member states to sell and buy each other's goods and services as if they were in the same country. Most of the members are in the EU, but there are ways Britain can leave the EU and retain the benefits of the single market – like Norway does.

There are some other European organisations that Britain could join instead of being in the EU. One of these is the European Free Trade Association. This is an independent grouping of non-EU nations who are mostly members of the single market.

So there are many options the government could take:

- Leave the EU and stay in the single market and the customs union
- Leave the single market but stay in the customs union
- Stay in the single market but leave the customs union
- Leave all three
- Leave with a trade deal
- Leave without a trade deal
- Join the European Free Trade Association and stay in the single market
- Join the European Free Trade Association and leave the single market
- Leave everything but maintain all existing policing and security arrangements as well as European coordination on disease control and nuclear materials
- End every single aspect of European cooperation and retreat behind the cliffs of Dover.

This mind-boggling list goes to the heart of the problem: the referendum settled a question, but it did not shape the answer.

Instead we are forced to try and extrapolate a particular type of Brexit from the result and the arguments made during the campaign. It's a messy, frustrating process, but it's all we have.

Take the central slogan of the Leave campaign: 'We send the EU £350 million a week. Let's fund our NHS instead.' The £350 million figure was misleading. It failed to mention the rebate negotiated by Margaret Thatcher or the funding that Europe sends back to Britain.

The NHS promise was dropped straight after the vote. But put that to one side for a moment. Politically, what does the success of a campaign trading on that £350 million slogan mean? That Britain must not send any money to the EU? Or just pay less?

There is a big difference between the two. If Britain left the EU but stayed in the single market, it would cut – but not end – its contribution to the EU budget. Is this enough? Or would it need to make sure that not a single penny went to the EU?

For many Leave voters, money was less important than sovereignty. Polling by the businessman Lord Ashcroft released shortly after the vote found the belief that 'decisions about the UK should be made in the UK' was the most popular argument among those who opted for Brexit. And it's undeniable that the Leave campaign's 'Take back control' slogan was effective. It encapsulated all sorts of issues, from financial contributions to the primacy of Parliament to border controls.

Others interpreted the result in a different way, saying it was a consequence of workers' sense of anger over stagnant wages since the financial crash in 2008. And it was true that most Labour constituencies voted Leave, although it is worth remembering that two-thirds of Labour voters backed Remain.

Ultimately, these were all symptoms of an underlying condition; of something much bigger and more profound. In one of the concluding paragraphs of *Well You Did Ask*, Ashcroft's book on the referendum, he says:

'Above all, whatever was printed on the ballot paper, the question large numbers of voters heard, and the reply they gave, was nothing much to do with the European Union. People tried to wrestle with such facts

as were available, and to make sense of the competing promises and claims. But ultimately, the question many saw was: 'Are you happy with the way things are and the way they seem to be going?' And their answer was: 'Well, since you ask... no'.

How do you respond to that mandate? What's the policy response to a fundamental rejection of the status quo? One thing is certain: politicians should not be trusted with such a big, messy question. They are, by their nature, ideologically self-serving. They will interpret events in a way which justifies whatever opinions they hold.

And that is precisely what happened. After the referendum, Nigel Farage, leader of the UK Independence Party, said voters had backed a points-based system for immigration. This went far beyond suggesting there was a mandate for ending or reforming free movement and into the realm of saying there was support for its specific replacement, which happened to be the one favoured by Nigel Farage. It served to demonstrate how enthusiastically politicians were suddenly ascribing a swell of popularity to whatever policy they happened to like that morning.

Meanwhile, Britain's newly installed Secretary of State for Exiting the European Union, David Davis, was claiming mandates for all sorts of things while unceremoniously dumping the £350 million NHS pledge which had been on the side of the campaign bus. Politicians had found a big old pot of electoral mandate and they were going to use it to paint any picture they damn well pleased.

Britain entered a political world with very few certainties, lots of emotions and a widespread feeling of democratic mission – a dangerous mix.

There had been a similar mixture of emotions and historic entitlement following the Scottish independence vote, but in that case, at least the SNP had put out a detailed white paper making clear what would happen in the case of victory. In the case of Brexit there was nothing but a collection of inaccurate and mutually incompatible statements made by various Brexiters.

One thing, though, was agreed by almost everyone. The Brexit vote had been a comprehensive rejection of freedom of movement: the right of citizens from any EU state to settle in the UK. This indeed was the main message the new prime minister, Theresa May, took from the result and there was much cross-party consensus to support her. Labour MPs reported there was rage about free movement on predominantly white council estates, just as Tory MPs returned from the shires with similar demands from the country golf club ringing in their ears. Very quickly a view took hold in the political class: the free movement of people was a symbol of a public sense of powerlessness. It must be ended.

In actual fact, this conclusion is questionable. Once you drill down into the Brexit mandate, something interesting happens: there is a split between those who want immigration reduced no matter the cost, and those who only want lower immigration if there is no economic cost. That is potentially important, because ending free movement will almost certainly entail leaving the single market. And leaving the single market is forecast by the overwhelming majority of experts to damage the British economy.

Shortly before the vote, an Ipsos Mori poll for Newsnight found 20% of Leave voters agreed with the statement:

'Britain should continue to allow European Union citizens to come to live and work in Britain in return for access to the EU single market.'

A poll by YouGov for the Adam Smith Institute in June 2016 found 42% of Leave voters thought Britain should pursue a Norway-style model inside the single market. An Ashcroft poll in the same month with a sample of 12,000 found 21% of Leave voters thought immigration was a force for good.

These results remained broadly the same after the referendum. An Ipsos Mori poll found 45% of Britons wanted single market membership prioritised in negotiations with the EU, over 39% who wanted immigration to be prioritised.

You find the same results in poll after poll after poll: somewhere between 20% and 40% of Leave voters are either indifferent to levels of immigration, or would not be prepared to see them cut if doing so hurt the economy.

Take that 20%-40% support away and Leave would not have won. Add it to the Remain vote and you have no mandate to end the free movement of people. So even here, in the one measure which is treated as unarguable, there is no clear mandate.

But regardless of its objective legitimacy, the necessity of lowering immigration is the most common interpretation of the Brexit vote. It has been accepted by most Labour and Tory MPs and has been embraced by anti-immigration tabloids. It has become received wisdom that something must be done about freedom of movement. It is a non-negotiable 'red line'.

The consequence is that Britain has only two options: to convince its EU partners to reform the rules on freedom of movement or leave the single market. It is arguably the biggest decision the UK has made since the end of the Second World War.

We mentioned several possible approaches to Brexit earlier, but in truth only one distinction matters: do we stay in the single market and customs union or not? That is the choice behind a soft or hard Brexit.

If Britain stays in the single market and customs union, the consequences of Brexit to most people's day-to-day lives are relatively modest. If we do not, the other connections we keep with the EU are barely relevant: the big decision has been made.

To many people, this may come as a surprise. There was very little mention during the campaign of the choices Britain would have to make. Instead, it was conducted in broad, colourful, almost childlike terms.

Leave wasn't an alternate economic or political model. It was a blank canvas onto which people could project their hopes, aspirations and frustrations. This was the only way you could get voters from the shires to vote with those from post-industrial towns in the north. It was a fantasy land of universal expectation.

This vague, laughably optimistic debate took place against a backdrop of social media echo chambers. Increasingly people were getting their news from Facebook, where they could tune out views they didn't agree with and create a constantly self-affirming information feed which only confirmed their pre-existing prejudices. Right-wing populists, trading in vivid and resonant stereotypes and dog-whistle messages on immigration, dominated the news agenda. By the end of the referendum campaign, truth counted for nothing.

And that wasn't just on the Leave side. Remain too issued some unhelpful, plainly self-interested warnings, like David Cameron's allusion to a third world war or George Osborne's pledge of a punishment Budget.

But undoubtedly the worst sins were committed by the Leave campaign, whose insiders readily admitted they had no interest in the facts. As Aaron Banks, the millionaire funder of Leave. EU said: 'Facts don't work. You have got to connect with people emotionally. It's the Trump success.'

After the referendum was over, acknowledging the difficulties we faced in leaving the EU was considered to show a lack of faith in Britain. Those in favour of Brexit closed their ears to discussions about complexity. A political culture took hold where baseless optimism was prized over sobriety.

Trade association bosses going to visit David Davis in the summer of 2016 were first ushered into a room by civil servants. There, they were briefed that they needed to go into the meeting saying that they were very excited by the possibilities of Brexit. Anyone who felt differently tended to be asked to leave in the first five minutes.

Now the Brexit ball of fuzzy mandate and heated emotion has crashed headfirst into an immovable object: European bureaucracy.

Welcome to Article 50.

What is Article 50?

Theresa May triggered Article 50 – the European Union rule that must be invoked by any country wishing to leave – on 29 March 2017. Unlike pretty much any other European law ever written, Article 50 is very short. Here it is in full (though you can skip it and continue reading):

1. Any Member State may decide to withdraw from the Union in accordance with its own constitutional requirements.

2. A Member State which decides to withdraw shall notify the European Council of its intention.

In the light of the guidelines provided by the European Council, the Union shall negotiate and conclude an agreement with that State, setting out the arrangements for its withdrawal, taking account of the framework for its future relationship with the Union.

That agreement shall be negotiated in accordance with Article 218(3) of the Treaty on the Functioning of the European Union.

It shall be concluded on behalf of the Union by the Council, acting by a qualified majority, after obtaining the consent of the European Parliament.

3. The Treaties shall cease to apply to the State in question from the date of entry into force of the withdrawal agreement or, failing that, two years after the notification referred to in paragraph 2, unless the European Council, in agreement with the Member State concerned, unanimously decides to extend this period.

4. For the purposes of paragraphs 2 and 3, the member of the European Council or of the Council representing the withdrawing Member State shall not participate in the discussions of the European Council or Council or in decisions concerning it.

A qualified majority shall be defined in accordance with Article 238(3)(b) of the Treaty on the Functioning of the European Union.

5. If a State which has withdrawn from the Union asks to rejoin, its request shall be subject to the procedure referred to in Article 49.

The important fact is that Article 50 is brutal. Insofar as it was ever expected to be used, it was as a punishment mechanism. 'I wrote Article 50, so I know it well,' the former Italian prime minister Giuliano Amato said shortly after the Brexit vote. 'My intention was that it should be a classic safety valve that was there, but never used.'

That can be demonstrated by the fact that Article 50 is functionally impossible, insanely restrictive and lacking in any detail; Amato put it into the Lisbon treaty specifically to counter British complaints that there was no way to escape the EU.

Article 50 will make any country that leaves the EU suffer. If another leader 'is as mad as Cameron' and offers a referendum on leaving the EU, Amato warned, they should know that: 'When it comes to the economy, they have to lose.'

Article 50 has all the signs of being jotted down on a single piece of A4, yet it is the process by which Britain is extricating itself from the largest trading bloc in the world.

The key provision is Clause 3 – that a departing state must leave the EU within two years of invoking Article 50. That deadline is awkward because leaving the EU requires three hellishly complicated processes. Britain must carry out an administrative Brexit, a legal Brexit, and an economic Brexit. In an ideal world, or even a desirable one, all three would be completed before a country left the EU. But this is not an ideal world.

Administrative Brexit

Administratively, we need to negotiate our outstanding commitments, which assets we're entitled to a share of, who pays off our MEPs and general British staff, our pension liabilities and a lot of other dull technicalities. Most contentious of these issues is the status of the 1.2 million British citizens living in the EU and the 3.2 million EU citizens living in the UK. David Davis intends to trade the rights of one for the other. His colleague, the International Trade Secretary Liam Fox, went so far as to call the EU migrants in the UK 'one of our main cards'.

The manner in which EU migrants have been discussed – as if they are a bargaining chip to be used rather than people to be respected – has been a low point in British public life. But quite apart from that moral inadequacy, it is not at all clear that the British ministerial team will be competent enough to secure a tit-for-tat legal recognition of both groups. As we shall see, so far they have proved utterly inept at exploiting their advantages.

Legal Brexit

Then there is the legal Brexit. As we shall see, this is a problem of horrific complexity. Britain has nearly half a century of entwined EU and UK law to sort out. The scale of it is almost beyond comprehension, and experts warn that it could take a decade or more to complete satisfactorily.

Trade Brexit

Should Britain stay in the single market and customs union, we will not need a trade deal. But if we leave them we will need some sort of post-Brexit trading arrangement with the EU, or we will see the return of tariffs and non-tariff barriers to our largest market.

People often assume that Article 50 covers administration, the law and trade. It actually covers only administration. The legal headache is Britain's problem. Trade agreements – which come under the euphemism 'future relationship' – are something the EU member states are only expected to be 'taking account of'.

'Taking account of' is wonderfully woolly phrase, giving the EU maximum flexibility. In reality it means that trade discussions are in Europe's gift. Britain petitioned Europe to allow administrative and future trade talks to take place simultaneously. Ministers even briefed journalists that Britain would insist on discussing trade talks from the start, but in the end London capitulated within hours of the first round of talks starting in June 2016. The structure of Article 50 puts Brussels firmly in control.

Given the scale of Brussels' discretionary powers, nurturing the EU's goodwill should have been vital to Britain. And that's why it was so jaw-droppingly unhelpful after the referendum for Nigel Farage to have made such a mean-spirited victory speech, in which he mocked MEPs: 'You're not laughing now, are you?' Several prominent British ministers also made aggressive comments about Brussels, helping to poison the attitude towards the UK team.

The outcome of Article 50 talks must be approved by the European Parliament, where MEPs decide laws, and the European Council, which comprises the heads of state of EU countries.

Finally there is the supreme European advantage: the time-scale, which stands at an improbable two years. The only way to extend it is with the unanimous agreement of the European Council. This may well be possible, but it is a big ask. Any of the 27 member states can veto a time extension. If member states see us with our back against the wall, facing the reality of a chaotic Brexit, they can leverage that advantage to negotiate concessions out of us. Again, EU nations dominate the leaving country.

Put simply, Article 50 is a diplomatic and legal horror story to keep civil servants awake at night. Although it has severe legal, economic and political consequences, it is conducted to an impossible timetable, with failure weighing disproportionately on the smaller negotiating partner. The larger negotiating partner, the EU, operates as both a single agent and as a collection of individual countries, each of which can influence the outcome at key moments.

Arguably the most severe problem Britain faces is the absence of trade experts and negotiators. Once Britain joined the customs union in 1973, the EU did the trade dealing for us. If you were a British trade negotiator, you went to Brussels.

It is difficult to recruit for these jobs. Britain urgently requires trade negotiators, analysts, statisticians and diplomats. It needs them both with a general background and specific expertise in areas like intellectual property and dispute settlement. These are difficult, often very boring areas and the people who specialise in them tend to have done so for their entire career. You can't just pluck a smart young thing from the civil service and train them up in a few weeks. They'll be eaten alive in negotiations. Ministers need them out the box, ready to go.

Coordination is a problem too. Negotiators must be armed with instructions on government policy across the board, from agriculture to electronic technical specifications to customs requirements to tariff rate quotas to government procurement to steel dumping. And, as we will see, to be successful they need to be doing this with the EU and the WTO simultaneously.

The instructions that this disparate army of experts receive will need to be very clear. And that means having a British leadership team in London with a specific and deliverable idea of what they are trying to achieve and how they will achieve it. Capacity isn't just about manpower; it's about intellectual power, too.

It is a coordination challenge on a near unimaginable scale. Nothing like this has been attempted before. There were places like Kosovo, which suddenly popped formally into existence and had to sort out all sorts of trading arrangements, but the comparison is not particularly useful. No advanced economy which is a central cog in the global financial system has attempted anything like Brexit.

After the referendum, Britain had about 40 people who could do the job. That is nothing like enough. Brexit requires hundreds of them. The EU has 550.

And Britain is not just negotiating with the EU. While Article 50 is ongoing, it also needs a B-team negotiating with the WTO, either as a fallback option or quite possibly as an ultimate destination. It also needs to be pursuing trade agreements, or at least preliminary talks, with countries like the US, China and Japan. It is the single biggest manpower crisis to hit the civil service in living memory.

The departmental framework for this project was only recently put in place. The moment that Theresa May walked into No. 10, she created a Department of International Trade, to be headed by her former leadership rival Liam Fox.

UK Trade and Investment, responsible for supporting British firms abroad and attracting inward investment, was folded into that new department, along with UK Export Finance, and the trade team at the Department for Business, Innovation and Skills – comprising just a handful of people, really. The trade team's job was to brief ministers on their options, but it was quickly overwhelmed. A call was put out for 300 trade advisers. New Zealand offered to chip in. Feelers were put out to the Canadians, who had just finalised a trade deal with the EU, asking if it had any trade negotiators at a loose end who might fancy some freelance work. Ministers are likely to have to hire management consultants from firms like McKinsey at what will be eye-watering prices. Step-by-step, a department has been bolted together, but without the experts needed to populate it.

Unlike Fox's Frankenstein's Monster of a department, the Department for Exiting the European Union headed by David Davis was made out of nothing and urgently started hiring. Civil servants – predominantly youngish well-educated Londoners were overwhelmingly Remain voters. At least initially, few fancied dedicating a core part of their career to delivering something they didn't support.

The third side of the triangle was the Foreign Office, which has long been considered the home of the most capable British civil servants. But its role in Brexit was mercurial. What would it really be doing? The fact that Boris Johnson was put in charge surprised many. Was he being put out to pasture in foreign fields, or did the prime minister envisage him sweet talking important world figures ahead of detailed negotiating work? It was unclear.

Cross-departmental coordination would be handled by the Cabinet Office. May made herself chair of three Cabinet Office committees covering every aspect of Brexit (The Economy and Industrial Strategy, International Trade, and Exiting the European Union), the last of which she packed with die-hard Brexiters alongside a few moderates.

Almost as soon as this structure was set up, divisions emerged between the Brexit ministers – Fox, Davis and Johnson, all eurosceptics and dubbed the Three Musketeers – on budgets and lines of accountability. This became more severe after Theresa May failed to win a general election in June 2017, leaving the Tory Party without a working majority in Parliament.

Unfortunately Britain's Brexit team lacks trade expertise or experience and works according to an overlapping departmental structure without clear lines of accountability.

Worst of all, the ministers who have shaped the government's approach to negotiations have gravely underestimated their negotiating partner.

What is the European project?

Britain has always been deeply ignorant of the motivation behind the European project. The most common British response to European politicians is indifference, followed by frustration, followed by mockery. But without understanding Europe, you can't effectively negotiate with Europe.

Ultimately, the European Union arose out of the ashes of the Second World War. In 1951, to prevent future disputes over resources, six nations agreed to trade freely in steel and coal. In 1957, the nations of the Coal and Steel Community (France, West Germany, Italy, Holland, Belgium and Luxembourg) signed the Treaty of Rome, founding the European Economic Community, which created a bigger common market and a customs union. Over time this common market attracted more nations and became the European Union.

For years Britain stood outside this club. In 1951, Prime Minister Clement Attlee declined an invitation to join the Coal and Steel Community, dismissing it as 'six nations, four of whom we had to rescue from the other two.' Britain also spurned the European Economic Community in 1958. While the European states looked to each other for peace and prosperity, the UK, with its still large empire and its special relationship with the

United States, gazed overseas. Britain and the Continent were divided not just by geography, but by conflict. A great deal of the British psyche derives from the fact that we have not been invaded for centuries. We went through incredible suffering during the world wars, but it fell from the sky. It did not march down the streets in jackboots. On the mainland, that trauma was and is personal: the social memory of a neighbour's betrayal, death camps, and tyranny. The EU is considered a barrier to conflict and carries an emotional weight we struggle to understand. Our MPs underestimate the resolve of Europe to preserve political unity.

Historically Britain has preferred to have a commercial relationship with the Continent. When Britain snubbed the coal and steel community, it started a looser trading club, the European Free Trade Association, with Austria, Denmark, Portugal, Sweden, Norway and Switzerland. Slowly Britain realised the European common market was booming and applied to join, but its entry was vetoed twice by French president Charles de Gaulle, which was frankly a little off given that London had offered him a place to stay during the war. Britain eventually got in in 1973 and held a referendum on membership a couple of years later, which was easily passed:

Do you think the UK should stay in the European Community (Common Market)?

YES 17,378,581 (67.23%)
NO 8,470,073 (32.77%)

During this period it was mostly the Left which was wary of European integration. It saw it as a free market initiative, which it was. But gradually the Right grew increasingly outraged by the federalist ambitions of many European officials. It wasn't paranoia either – EU leaders really were out to create a federal state of Europe. Then, in 1987, the single market was born. It was everything sceptics of the European project feared it would be.

What is the single market?

The single market had been the dream of European planners from the outset. It would not just get rid of tariffs like an ordinary free trade agreement, it would create four fundamental freedoms:

- **Goods**
- **Capital**
- **Services**
- **People**

The people and businesses of Europe would merge into one system. Companies could sell their products anywhere, money could flow freely, professional services like insurance or advertising could be offered across the Continent, and people would be free to work and live wherever they wanted, whenever they wanted. These powers were interlinked. After all, what was the point of ensuring qualifications for services like dentistry or hairdressing were recognised all over the Continent if people couldn't travel to sell them?

For this to happen, EU nations had to transfer lots of powers to Brussels. A single market required its members to standardise regulations: competition could only happen if everyone played by the same rules.

Take Cassis de Dijon, a little blackcurrant liqueur with an alcohol content of between 15% and 20%. It sounds dreadful, but the French really like it. Germany used to have a law requiring all fruity alcohol drinks to have at least 25% alcohol, so it banned Cassis de Dijon. Previously Germany would have been able to dictate which goods were sold in its territory, but no longer. Europe ruled that Germany had unlawfully restricted the free movement of goods.

This is how the single market works: it standardises markets. It doesn't really affect domestic law in other parts of society, like health or crime, but it tells firms what standards they have to meet and forces countries to take those products, regardless of whether governments or companies want them. This recognition of standards reflects a key part of what makes trade work. It is something which presents one of the greatest dangers to Britain when it pulls away from Europe: non-tariff barriers.

In recent years, as tariffs have eroded away, non-tariff barriers have come to preoccupy the thoughts of trade experts. Non-tariff barriers are obstacles to trade outside of taxation. Some are insurmountable, like language. Others are not.

Mutual recognition agreements are key to overcoming some of these problems. When two countries sign these agreements they acknowledge each other's standards and paperwork on product testing and conformity in areas of their economy. There are various degrees of recognition. Sometimes they say that any product a country makes in a certain sector, like telecoms, is recognised by the other nation. Sometimes they are little more than priority lanes at customs checkpoints for recognised producers. Either way, they are part of the patchwork of arrangements that allows trade to flow freely around the world. Losing these agreements leads to tailbacks at the border.

But it doesn't stop there. The EU also has mutual recognition agreements with other major economies. If Britain leaves the single market it does not just lose recognition with Europe. It is likely to lose it with many of the countries that trade with Europe. The EU has these agreements with Australia, Canada, China, Israel, Japan, New Zealand, the United States and Switzerland. When Brexiters say that they want to leave Europe to trade with the rest of the world, they fail to realise that leaving Europe is an obstacle to trading with the rest of the world.

The rules on standards within the single market extend to all products a country makes – not just those exported to Europe. And they dig deep. They go from the information you need to put on food packaging to noise levels on a lawnmower.

They don't just apply to the finished product either. They apply to the labour that went into it. It's the only way to have a level playing field. If two countries both have to build products to a set specification but one can make workers do 72 hours a week and the other only 48, it's pretty obvious which one will pull ahead. So working conditions are set at a certain level across the single market, as are environmental regulations. The intention is to make Europe trade as if it were a single entity.

This is where all the screaming tabloid headlines about straight bananas and the like come from. Many of them are true and startling in their bureaucratic nitpicking. Many of them are entirely reasonable attempts to smooth out standards and help consumers.

The most notable exponent of the Brussels-bureaucracy-gone-mad story was none other than Boris Johnson, the Brussels correspondent of the *Daily Telegraph* between 1989 and 1994. Prior to Johnson's arrival, Brussels correspondents had been filing lifeless copy on procedural issues. By the time Johnson was finished, Brussels reports had turned into a journalistic genre – a daily diet of half-true stories about faceless bureaucrats and rigid conformity stifling British ingenuity.

'Everything I wrote from Brussels, I found was sort of chucking these rocks over the garden wall,' Johnson reminisced later. 'And I listened to this amazing crash from the greenhouse next door over in England as everything I wrote from Brussels was having this amazing, explosive effect on the Tory party, and it really gave me this I suppose rather weird sense of power.' You can see the germ of Johnson's later role in the Brexit campaign: the emotional detachment, the vague sense that he doesn't really believe what he's saying, and the canny understanding of how to use Europe to influence Conservative sentiment.

Many businesses did find the single market rules stifling, especially small businesses that were forced to produce to a European standard despite only selling locally. Others found them liberating. Financial and regulatory impediments to trade fell away, allowing businesses to send employees all over the Continent without getting bogged down in endless bureaucracy over visas. They banished, seemingly forever, the costly irritations of tariffs and non-tariff barriers.

There were and are complaints. Arguably the single market contributed to a sense that people had lost any power at work and were forced to follow rules made not by themselves, nor their bosses, nor even their company, but by people they'd never meet in an obscure city they would never visit. They were also much harsher on small businesses than big ones.

But the economic advantages were considerable and lots of people wanted to share them. Take the European Free Trade Association (EFTA), the organisation which Britain founded back in 1960 and then left. In 1994 EFTA's four remaining members – Iceland, Liechtenstein, Norway and Switzerland – signed a deal with the European Union to create the European Economic Area (EEA). In essence, those countries were allowed to join the single market without being in the EU. It is because of this agreement that a soft Brexit is even possible. It provides a potential safety net by which Britain can leave the European Union and stay in the single market.

But this might not be straightforward, as Switzerland, which also has a prickly relationship with the EU, found out. The government wanted to be part of the European Economic Area, but the Swiss model of mixed representative and direct democracy forced it to hold a referendum. The public rejected EEA membership. The Swiss government went into damage-limitation mode and stitched together a series of bilateral deals which gave access to, but not membership of, the single market. It's a messy, bespoke, halfway house solution, which we'll deal with later.

People talk about the EU and the single market as if they are the same thing. But they are not. The EU is the body which created and manages the single market, but it is distinct from it. You can leave the EU and stay in the single market.

That does, though, come with a big drawback. EFTA countries like Norway or Switzerland have to follow single market rules but don't have any formal say in formulating them. If you are not a member of the club, you do not get a seat at the table. Nonetheless, the economic area deal allowed countries wary of the European project, with all its federalist talk of ever-closer union, to stay safely outside the EU while enjoying the economic benefits.

It could be a way out for Britain, but it will be difficult, because of the nature of British and European politics.

What are the politics of the European Union?

Successive waves of enlargements have increased the EU. Currently it has 28 members (Diagram 1, below):

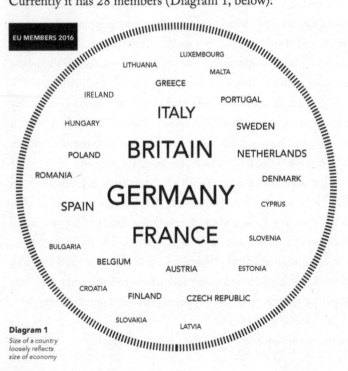

EU MEMBERS 2016

LITHUANIA
LUXEMBOURG
MALTA
GREECE
IRELAND
PORTUGAL
ITALY
HUNGARY
SWEDEN
POLAND
BRITAIN
NETHERLANDS
ROMANIA
DENMARK
GERMANY
SPAIN
CYPRUS
FRANCE
BULGARIA
SLOVENIA
BELGIUM
AUSTRIA
ESTONIA
CROATIA
FINLAND
CZECH REPUBLIC
SLOVAKIA
LATVIA

Diagram 1
Size of a country
loosely reflects
size of economy

In the 1990s, the EU constructed the Eurozone, a monetary union of 19 member states using the euro as currency. It also created the Schengen Area, which abolished passport controls and other border checks between their countries.

Let's look at the nucleus of EU states who have the euro. These are the countries keenest on European integration, or at least, those keenest to share their currency with Germany.

As you can see from Diagram 2, Britain is not there. The UK did not join the Eurozone or the Schengen area. That may have been a good move, certainly in the case of the Eurozone. The project was set up with the sort of heady sense of historic

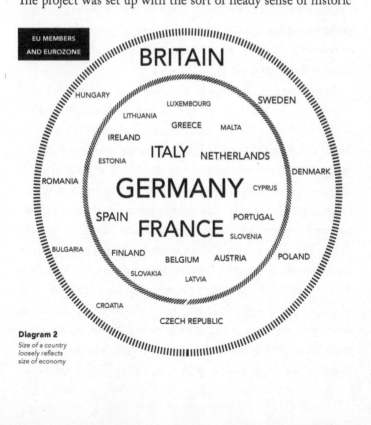

EU MEMBERS AND EUROZONE

BRITAIN

HUNGARY

LUXEMBOURG

SWEDEN

LITHUANIA

GREECE

MALTA

IRELAND

ITALY

NETHERLANDS

ESTONIA

ROMANIA

GERMANY

CYPRUS

DENMARK

SPAIN

PORTUGAL

FRANCE

SLOVENIA

BULGARIA

FINLAND

BELGIUM

AUSTRIA

POLAND

SLOVAKIA

LATVIA

CROATIA

CZECH REPUBLIC

Diagram 2
Size of a country loosely reflects size of economy

preordination with which many Brexiters now treat the UK's exit from the EU. Warnings of fundamentally incompatible economies and German control were ignored in an almost religious belief in the importance of melding countries together and a bizarre, but at the time largely unquestioned, assumption of permanent economic growth. Greece eventually suffered a debt crisis, and was forced into a form of perpetual servitude by its creditors. The dream of united statehood started to look more like tyranny.

The reality of the Eurozone project has been high unemployment and slow growth. The most obvious comparison is with the Soviet Union in the 1970s and '80s. Public support for any project would be eroded by years of sluggish performance, lack of competitiveness, and an unresponsive political system – and Europe is no exception.

In the case of Schengen, the dream of borderless travel has started to fall apart in the face of a seemingly endless wave of refugees fleeing war, poverty, and oppression in the Middle East and North Africa. The scale and speed of this influx has caused tensions across the EU. Italy and Greece, because of their geographical location, are the first port of call for migrants arriving in Europe, but other member states have not been prepared to contribute sufficient resources to help them. The increasingly violent response by police in eastern European states angered their western partners, but there has been no practical assistance to accompany their criticism.

Germany's decision to welcome a million refugees was an act of extraordinary political bravery, but it prompted resentment from countries on the migration trail and destabilised the domestic political base of its Chancellor, Angela Merkel.

These twin crises – debt and refugees – created a surge of euroscepticism on the Continent. More than ever before, people questioned the European project. It was a component, perhaps, of a broader global trend, finding its most grotesque expression in the election of Donald Trump as US President. Populists – typically of the right but occasionally of the left – proved adept at channelling anger over stagnating wages, economic insecurity and globalisation into an attack on the status quo and an affirmation of national, religious or cultural identity. So far there have been no European electoral shocks to compare with Brexit and Trump, but the underlying tensions remain. And they could return.

Brussels has been terrible at making its case. It has persistently failed to show how it helps the public. Think for instance of the 56% Leave vote in Cornwall, which will receive £2.5 billion from the EU between 2000 and 2020, and which also benefits from the legal protections on Cornish pasties. Without any coverage of the benefits of the EU, the press is free to fixate on the negatives. And there are plenty of those, from trade deals with secret corporate courts, to an instinctive indifference to the nation state, to petty or over-zealous regulation.

Few citizens understand the democratic structures of the European Union. It has three working parts:

- **the Commission**
- **the Parliament**
- **the Council**

The Commission proposes and writes laws. The laws are debated, scrutinised and voted on in the Parliament by MEPs elected by the public. The Council is made up of ministers from each member state. It scrutinises laws before they are enacted.

So you have one unelected body thinking up and writing laws and two elected bodies – one directly and one indirectly – scrutinising it. It's a pretty good system for scrutiny, but it's also a bit shady.

People struggle to describe the Commission. What is it exactly? A government? A civil service? Something in between? Supporters of the EU will tell you that civil servants write legislation all the time in the UK, so we should not be outraged when the same thing happens in Brussels. That's true, but civil servants don't propose it – ministers do. And those ministers ran for government on the back of a manifesto which was supported by voters at the ballot box. You can get rid of Labour or the Conservatives, but you can't get rid of the European Commission.

These bodies don't function particularly smoothly either. Much of the time they're eyeing each other up suspiciously. Occasionally they are in open warfare. The Commission and the Council even had a territorial dispute over who would take the lead in Brexit negotiations.

These clashes take place amid a growing demand from member states for more control. The approval of a recent Canada-EU trade deal – negotiated over seven years – was put in jeopardy when member states were involved in its ratification. That wasn't a legal requirement but a political one. It reflected a growing confidence and even belligerence among member states.

Voters across Europe feel frustrated with Brussels and its

seemingly remote and arcane institutions. No ordinary voter would ever tune in to see a debate take place in the European Parliament. Its scrutiny systems are only of interest to policy wonks and even then it is pretty tough going. There is no prime minister's question time, in which political debate bursts into life and the public can see someone being held to account. It becomes easy for politicians and the press to blame Brussels for everything, because no-one sees it doing anything.

This is partly the result of having an international decision-making body and a national press. But Brussels must be at least partly responsible. It does not give people a reason to watch what goes on there.

When it does want to get a story out about itself it goes to the press corps, but these reporters struggle to reach the public. They are typically more concerned with figuring out the arcane details of EU law-making than with colourful, impactful journalism. The average Brussels correspondent has just about mastered how the milk quotas work, but no normal person has read their stories for years. Boris Johnson did more to influence public opinion with one of his imaginary stories about the rules on bananas than the average EU correspondent has done in their entire career.

Despite these limitations Brussels mostly managed to stare down the recent rise in euroscepticism. Brexiters dreamt that their project would trigger the collapse of the EU, but it actually seemed to reaffirm many Europeans' commitment to the project. Look under the surface, though, and many danger remain.

Places like Finland, Sweden and Denmark, which were once reliable supports of the European project, have now flirted with euroscepticism. Spain saw its economy deteriorate and unemployment spiral as part of Europe's economic convulsions. In Greece the cruel financial straitjacket imposed by its creditors has condemned the country to poverty without any hope of an end. In Austria, antagonism to the political elite led to a Green and a fascist running for the Presidency (the Green won). In Italy a clown, Beppe Grillo, set the political agenda.

In each place euroscepticism has a regional flavour but its underlying emotional content is the same. In Eastern Europe the broiling anger and dissatisfaction is markedly different to what is seen in England but it has the same political DNA: a desire to pull up borders, a distrust of the present, a romanticisation of the past. In Poland, Hungary, the Czech Republic, Slovakia and other former communist states there is frustration they were forced to implement rapid free-market reforms and fall into line with western Europe's commercial and cultural standards. That left-wing nostalgia sits next to a right-wing fury over perceived 'cultural poisoning' from immigration.

These countries feel that they have been pushed around. They naively thought that swapping the Communist empire for the European Union would mean they could do what they liked, but they quickly discovered that the EU is a highly rules-based organisation. Culturally, many of the policies they were steamrollered into might not have been quite right for them, but the EU turned a deaf ear. Western Europe's ability to sell into their countries through the single market was treated as a great boom, but it often caused unemployment and problems in housing and transport.

When eastern European states tried to object they found that Brussels' democratic mechanisms were pretty inhuman. They were ushered into Council meetings and told in no uncertain terms that the vote would go according to the majority. Could they vote against the proposal? Sure, they could. But they were going to lose. This sense of resentment against stronger neighbours is partly why these countries are instinctively critical of any Brexit brake on free movement. They know that when the UK complains about immigration, it isn't concerned about German architects, and that any change to freedom of movement based on skills, sector or income would turn eastern Europeans into second-class citizens.

Even in Germany and France, the two countries whose bonds formed the embryo of the European project after 1945, euroscepticism has grown. A candidate who wanted to leave the EU, Marine Le Pen, made the final round of the French presidential election. In the end, her campaign came to nothing. Emmanuel Macron, an avid supporter of the EU, won the final round, set back the march of euroscepticism and rejuvenated the Franco-German alliance – which is newly determined to show that the EU can work for its citizens. But many believe Le Pen will try again if eurosceptic tempers rise in the future. In Germany, a surprisingly robust performance by the hard right Alternative for Deutschland has left Angela Merkel looking vulnerable and focussed on domestic concerns.

The growth of euroscepticism, and the desire of keen Europeans to stop it in its tracks, explains the hostility on the Continent which Britain has met since the vote. Europe is on a damage limitation exercise – and we are the damage.

The first formal notice of the severity with which Europe intends to treat Britain came when the European Parliament appointed federalist Guy Verhofstadt as its Brexit representative. Verhofstadt previously branded Nigel Farage's salary the

EU's 'biggest waste of money' and, after the Brexit referendum, described Farrage, David Cameron and Boris Johnson as 'rats fleeing a sinking ship'. Verhofstadt is a hate figure for the euro-sceptic British tabloids and it's true that he was a particularly divisive and combative person to have chosen.

But there's marginally more subtlety to him. He is an advocate of offering countries associate status 'with less obligations but equally less rights' while the rest of the EU consolidates. Quite what that associate status would entail is another matter entirely. If it included restrictions on immigration it would not offer much market access, but this is an avenue for the British team to pursue and it suggests that the former Belgian prime minister is more flexible than he might sometimes appear.

Over at the European Commission, which is taking the day-to-day lead on the talks, Michel Barnier is in charge of Brexit negotiations, although he is acting on the mandate given to him by the Council. The French politician has long been considered anti-British by some elements of the UK press and that attitude was reflected in the coverage of his clashes with the British government over the City of London when he became the internal market commissioner. The anti-British accusation is nonsense. Barnier had come to develop a sympathy for British teams and a belief that they would deliver on what they agreed, although that sympathy may now have been tested to its limit by the behaviour of the UK delegation during Article 50 talks.

In the background, things look troubling for British negotiators. Commission President Jean-Claude Juncker and European Parliament President Martin Schulz both feel that the EU is at an historic moment and is battling to stay afloat amid a daily slew of bad news. Divisions between these two Brussels veterans are common, but they are much closer than people realise. They are said by European Parliament insiders to talk on the phone several times a day, including first thing in the morning and last thing at night.

That sense of unity isn't evident everywhere. The Council and the Commission were locked in a legal battle over who took the lead in Brexit talks. Many member states are uncomfortable that federalists like Juncker and Verhofstadt have taken such leading roles. Europe is not much less confused than we are. But that does not make the situation equal. EU states have a stranglehold on the negotiation process and disproportionate strength in their trading capacity.

Europe has proved adept at holding a uniform line on negotiations among all partners and rebuffing Britain's appeals for preliminary meetings. The first meeting without the UK took place shortly after the referendum result, with the second in Bratislava in September 2016. EU leaders made good use of their ability to exclude the UK from meetings where negotiating strategy was discussed. That exclusion happened all the way down the system. British MEPs reported being frozen out of meetings in every part of the EU. On the ground, the separation had already begun.

When Britain triggered Article 50 in March 2017, EU leaders had already had nine months to settle their aims and strategy. They were impressively transparent and well organised, putting out detailed position papers on a range of issues. Their guidelines severely restricted what Britain could hope to achieve once the talks began.

By contrast, Britain's approach was muddled and weak. Deciding when to trigger Article 50 was one of the few bits of leverage in the UK's hands. But Theresa May gave it away in October 2016, seemingly as an afterthought, during a Sunday morning interview ahead of the Conservative Party conference. Then — having already given it away — she tried to leverage it, by asking Europe for preliminary talks.

If the European Union had allowed preliminary talks it would have blunted two of its key advantages: firstly, the two-year deadline set in train by Article 50, and secondly its legal control on the subject matter of the talks. The EU is out to protect itself and is no longer interested in doing the UK any favours. May's decision to give away the date and then ask for talks was like an armed robber throwing down his weapon and demanding the bank staff surrender. Unsurprisingly, Europe did not comply. And there was more than a hint of frustration in Tusk's response.

This casual misjudgement suggested May shared the ignorance that British politicians have had about Brussels for decades. The British press almost never carries out a sober, judicious assessment of the EU. For the right, it is a tyranny in waiting, a crude Bonapartist force taking control of Europe. For the left, it is a beacon of internationalism, support for which is considered a test of progressive values.

Both views are hopelessly misguided. In reality, the European Union is a well-meaning but internally contradictory experiment in transnational political organisation. For everything that is sensible about it, there is something absurd. And for everything regrettable about it, there is something commendable. It is democratically flawed, but also nothing like as monstrous or opaque as its critics maintain.

The failure to assess it as a working organisation rather than a demonic fantasy means the government ministers in charge of Brexit are struggling to construct a credible negotiating strategy. During the referendum campaign, David Davis was telling audiences that EU member states could sign their own trade deals – something they have not had the power to do since the customs union was founded. If you don't know who you're negotiating with, it is hard to adopt the right tactics to get what you want from them.

At its simplest, the EU is a machine composed of three layers: trade, law and politics. Trade forms the mechanism which keeps everything moving. The law is the instruction manual which lays out how to keep the machine working smoothly. And the people operating the machine are the politics.

Britain went into negotiations with the EU with three key objectives. Firstly, it wanted to end freedom of movement. Secondly, it wanted to maintain or improve its current economic performance. Finally, it wanted to keep the United Kingdom intact.

Now let's see what happens when these demands are fed into the Brussels machine.

What will we do about freedom of movement?

European leaders have been vociferous in saying that there will be no compromise on freedom of movement. Immediately after the referendum, Jean-Claude Juncker said there would be no 'nuances' for the UK. A statement released by the 27 remaining European leaders stressed that access to the single market 'requires acceptance of all four freedoms'. Angela Merkel told the German parliament: 'If you wish to have free access to the single market then you have to accept the fundamental European rights.' Standing next to May outside the Élysée Palace, the then French President Francois Hollande stated: 'There cannot be freedom of movement of goods, free movement of capital, free movement of services if there isn't a free movement of people.'

When Boris Johnson joked that he was 'pro having my cake and pro eating it', Donald Tusk replied: 'To all who believe in it, I propose a simple experiment. Buy a cake, eat it, and see if it is still there on the plate.' The message is clear: there will be no movement on free movement. It is a European red line.

But there may be more wriggle room than the EU is making out. Brussels is bound to hold a firm line publicly, but ultimately the EU is good at making deals. As an organisation, its instinct is to sit down for very long and very boring talks and end up with a compromise that no-one is particularly happy about but which everyone can live with. And, as we'll see, there are strong economic and security reasons why it might want to keep Britain inside the tent. Or at least not fully outside the tent.

Look closely and you can see gaps in its red line on free movement. Shortly after the referendum, the influential Brussels-based Bruegal think tank released a report arguing that the EU should concede on this point. Unlike freedom of goods, services and capital, the principle of free movement of people was polit-ical, not economic, it argued. Interestingly, Norbert Rottgen, a former German federal minister and current chairman of the Bundestag's committee on foreign affairs, signed the document.

Around the same time, an unnamed high-ranking UK official told *The Observer* newspaper that an emergency brake on immi-gration was 'certainly one of the ideas now on the table'. Nick Clegg and Tony Blair have both said that EU officials expected to negotiate free movement after the referendum result and were surprised by the silence from Theresa May.

It's hardly enough to give you confidence in a change of course, but it does show that, behind the scenes of the public statements, there is more potential for compromise than one might think.

If a deal were to be offered, what would it be?

An emergency brake is the most likely. This might take the form of a pause on freedom of movement for, say, seven or ten years or perhaps a limit on numbers – keeping European immi-gration below 50,000 annually for a number of years. (In 2015, 270,000 EU citizens moved to the UK.)

An emergency break would be relatively easy for Europe to tolerate, because it would be temporary and not break any treaties. Brussels might find it difficult to justify because objectively there is no emergency. We have fewer new arrivals per head than other EU states and there is no solid evidence that they are a burden on welfare, public services or GDP, despite the tabloid scare stories. But EU lawyers could invent some system which fits the desired outcome. Its temporary nature should allow it to be approved by the Council and the Parliament. But would Brexiters accept it?

The answer to that is probably no. Prominent Tory MPs sense that this is their opportunity to sever the link with Europe once and for all. They feel the wind in their sails. Any temporary measure – which is precisely what would make this plan palatable to Europe – would probably make it unacceptable to them.

So what else might happen? Every so often European figures whisper about a more radical initiative to cauterise euroscepticism once and for all. Perhaps Brussels could return to the original Treaty of Rome which set up the EU, like some academic reinterpreting a biblical text, and use it to show the way forward. The wording in the treaty is interesting. It only mentions freedom of movement in relation to workers. In effect this is freedom of labour. You have the right to go to another country to work, subject to tests.

European case law has gradually expanded this, allowing EU citizens a few months once they arrive in a country to find work. But there is still a limit. Recent court cases in Germany have repatriated Romanians who failed to look for work before claiming benefits.

Some people – all of them optimists – believe this might offer a solution to the current predicament. Perhaps the need to find a job within a few months could be enshrined in a treaty? That wouldn't actually change anything as such: it would simply codify the limitations on free movement in a formal international document rather than in case law. Having a clear rule across Europe might assuage the concerns of France's National Front, Alternative for Germany and the others. Perhaps it could be tightened even further so people may only move to another country if they have a job offer? That would even remove the three-month window.

None of this is impossible, but it is improbable. It is hard to imagine Europe agreeing such a far-reaching initiative, at least within the Article 50 timetable. And it is unclear whether it would even be accepted in the UK. After all, freedom to work or move are the same when your red line is regaining control over the border. It's possible – or at least just about imaginable – that this plus a seven year pause would be enough for Leave supporters. But it is a stretch.

There is another, more radical idea brewing on the Continent. It is an idea that is not yet fully formed, whose time has not yet come, and which is unlikely to come within the timetable offered by Article 50. But it is there. It has different names, because it is presently more of an aspiration than an idea. Guy Verhofstadt calls it 'associate status'. The Bruegel paper called it 'continental partnership'. Others call it 'auxiliary status'. Still others theorise about a plan to allow UK industrial sectors to 'dock' with institutions in the European Economic Area, allowing some form of carve out for bits of the economy.

All these plans have at their foundation the universally accepted need for a 'two-speed Europe'. This can be seen as the manifestation of Continent-wide euroscepticism on one hand and Franco-German consolidation on the other.

In a sense, Europe is already operating at two speeds: the Eurozone countries are melding, while the rest hang back. But Brexit and the EU's other challenges have intensified the pressure for change.

Any creation of secondary status membership would probably entail a new treaty and a constitutional convention. This would take much longer than Article 50 allows, although it could fit within the timetable if British is forced to extend it, or if there were a long transitional arrangement. If this type of membership took account of British demands, for instance on free movement and budget contributions, Britain might accept it, although it wouldn't actually amount to Brexit. We would stay in the European Union, albeit under very different terms.

None of this is very realistic, though. The number of people who would need to agree is too high, and the time it would take would probably make it impractical.

The British plan is quite different. Ministers would like to replace free movement with a general system of work permits. At its most liberal, this plan would be similar to freedom of labour. Britain would issue work permits to anyone who has the offer of a job in the UK. That might get a fair hearing in Europe. Britain would still struggle to retain single market membership, but would probably have extensive access to the single market. Ministers would be able to tell the British public that they had taken back control of the border.

It is unlikely hardline Brexiters would be satisfied with this, however. They would prefer a sector-by-sector work permit system. High-income, high-skill workers would be allowed into the UK. Low-income, low-skill workers would not. Free movement for bankers, passport control for plumbers. This option would also allow the government to create exemptions for low-pay industries which struggle to find British workers, such as fruit picking, where there could be seasonal permits.

This deal is unlikely to appeal to Europe. EU leaders might accept it at a stretch, but with significantly reduced access to the single market. The gap between the Brexiters' position and that of EU leaders is so vast it is hard to imagine anything bridging it.

What about the economy?

The EU has a full range of menu options for the single market. Norway, for instance, has full membership of the single market; Switzerland has access to the single market through its painful bilateral treaties. Neither option is likely to happen. Opening the 2016 Conservative conference with a Brexit speech aimed at pleasing right-wingers in her party, Theresa May all but ruled out any form of single market membership. She went much further than just freedom of movement.

She said: 'We are not leaving the European Union only to give up control of immigration all over again. And we are not leaving only to return to the jurisdiction of the European Court of Justice. That's not going to happen. We're going to be able to make our own decisions on how we label our food.'

These three comments made continued membership of the single market almost impossible. Free movement, European court jurisdiction and product harmonisation are all essential to membership of the single market.

A highly technical reading of the speech might still have kept the UK in the single market. The European Free Trade Association does actually have its own court for the European Economic Area states, so Britain could join it while still sticking to the letter of her promise to leave the European Court of Justice. But this EFTA court must take account of European Court of Justice rulings, so the difference is largely superficial.

And anyway, the comment on food labelling seemed to rule it out. No matter which court you're with or what type of single market membership you have, you don't get to make your own decisions on how to label food. By stating this, May was going beyond the specific systems to a rejection of any interference in British regulation.

It was an odd thing to have said. As we shall see, Britain could not satisfy these goals even outside of the EU — unless it also planned to leave the World Trade Organisation. Standards of packaging apply at that level, so unless Britain plans to give up the concept of international trade in a North Korean model of complete isolation, she was going to have to break her promise.

That was the trouble with feeding Britain's political demands into the EU machine: they don't go in. Most British politicians seem to want the benefits of the single market without the requirements. It is equivalent to saying you want to go to Hungary but will refuse to abide by Hungarian law.

May's demands could not be delivered without real economic pain. But despite this, they were accepted by the vast majority of her colleagues. Although there were debates about relative levels of hard and soft Brexit, hardly anyone in the Conservative parliamentary party has questioned the plan to leave the single market and the customs union. Oddly, this basic assumption has also been accepted by the leadership of the Labour Party.

Nevertheless, it's worth looking more deeply into the existing models for being a member of the single market outside of the

EU, because they are all perfectly viable options for Britain, even now – and offer considerably more stability and less risk than the alternatives. Understanding them frames our comprehension of the advantages and disadvantages of Britain's options.

There may be more practical reasons, too. Economic concerns can quickly change the political consensus. After the referendum, the value of sterling plummeted, inflation rose, consumer debt spiralled, investment fell, and companies started re-locating overseas. A dramatic downturn could make staying in the single market more attractive to MPs and increase demands from the public for a change of course. Brexiters clearly have no wish to stay in, but that doesn't mean they won't be forced to.

Now we need another diagram to understand the different options. (Diagram 3 opposite)

Diagram 3

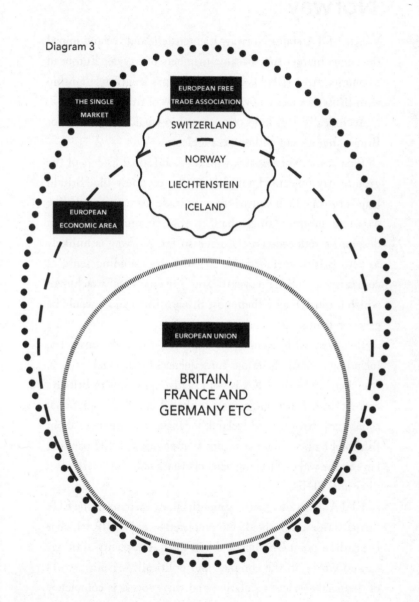

THE SINGLE MARKET

EUROPEAN FREE TRADE ASSOCIATION

SWITZERLAND

NORWAY

LIECHTENSTEIN

ICELAND

EUROPEAN ECONOMIC AREA

EUROPEAN UNION

BRITAIN, FRANCE AND GERMANY ETC

Norway

When EFTA states Norway, Lichtenstein and Iceland joined the single market they became members of a wider European Economic Area (EEA), securing an arm's length relationship with Brussels while enjoying the benefits of free trade.

Technically, this kind of relationship would be possible for Britain, but it's not without its problems.

Firstly, the Norwegians, who act as informal leaders of the group, may object. Having a massive economy like Britain leap into your little out-of-the-way trade arrangement is like someone dumping an elephant in your swimming pool. But despite its reticence on the issue so far, Norway is unlikely to veto British membership. It still has an abiding sense of comradeship to Britain over the war – an emotional attachment which is much bigger than most Brits realise – and it would be excessively impolite.

But even with Norwegian approval, there are obstacles, including potentially serious consequences to financial services. Membership of the EEA is not exactly equivalent to Britain's current deal. The arrangements in the EEA reflect its national economies. Norway and Iceland, for instance, care more about fish than banks. This has meant that changes to EU banking laws in the wake of the financial crisis are only now starting to filter into EFTA.

EFTA states are month by month taking on more of the EU's financial rules. This should be completed by early 2019, which is the earliest point Britain could join them. But plenty of things can go wrong in the complex and politically sensitive world of financial services regulation and this process is completely outside of the UK's control. If it got held up, British firms would lose passporting rights on the Continent regardless of our EEA membership.

Passporting allows a bank to sell a type of financial product across Europe. Some 5,500 City firms hold 330,000 passports. The most important stem from the EU Markets and Financial Instruments Directive, which allows groups to sell investments from one EU state to another. That's crucial for the City: it allows a bank in London to sell a French investor a mutual fund established in Dublin or Luxembourg. If the bank is unable to sell that product from London, it will have to accept less business or, more likely, start moving that part of its business to a country inside the single market.

There are other aspects of the deal which are unappealing. EEA countries are in an almost servile state next to the legislative force of the EU. They must accept the rules the EU passes about the single market, but they cannot influence them.

This is why the Norway model has such a bad name. It looks passive and desperate, a powerless hanger-on to a massive economic giant, wimpishly abiding by the rules of the larger partner: a little fish nibbling food off the skin of a shark.

But there are many more positives in Norway's arrangement than people like to admit and it has far more influence in shaping regulations than people realise. There is a reason no-one really comprehends its full complexity and opportunity – neither supporters nor opponents of the European Union want to acknowledge them.

To admit to the degree of influence Norway enjoys would mean Brexiters would have to confess that there are very significant restrictions on sovereignty outside the single market. For Remainers, any admission that Norway enjoys considerable influence would have undone their hard line during the campaign that only full EU membership is in Britain's national interest.

And for journalists and politicians it would mean admitting to the existence of a massive body of international standards that few understand or are even aware of.

Norway does something rather clever with its position in the European Free Trade Association. It goes above the head of the EU, to the global regulatory plane, and influences standards there. These standards then float down to the EU level.

One study concluded that when you strip out the international standards adopted by Brussels, only 8% of genuinely EU-originated law arrives in Norway. The majority of the 'EU law' accepted by Norway actually starts in international standards that have been adopted by the European Union.

The EU has an obligation to cooperate with a large number of global bodies, including the United Nations and its agencies, the Organisation for Security and Cooperation in Europe, the Organisation for Economic Cooperation and Development, International Maritime Organisation and the International Labour Organisation. These bodies are constantly churning out technical regulations, standards, testing and certification, which make up 33% of the EU's remit.

Another 28% of the EU's remit is 'veterinary and phytosanitary matters' – meaning animal and plant health for food trading. It's another area where much of the regulation comes down on from on high and is not much more than rubberstamped by the EU.

Many of the scare stories you've read about 'EU regulation gone mad' are actually about laws that originated above the EU's head. In 2013, for instance, there was a tabloid panic attack about an EU programme which removed the Union Flag from packets of meat. That actually came from the Codex Alimentarius, a collection of internationally recognised standards and codes of practice for food production. The EU had cut and pasted parts of the text into its regulation. But even the Codex wasn't original: it was relying on the World Trade Organisation's agreement on rules of origin.

The tabloids shouldn't have blamed Brussels at all, they should have blamed the Codex, except that the public has never heard of it, so it wouldn't have made a good story. The Codex and the WTO do not make useful bogey men, so the way their standards infringe on our supposedly much prized British sovereignty is rarely mentioned.

Britain implemented that flag rule through the EU, but when the next rule comes in it will be outside the EU, so it will implement it directly. Either way, the outcome will be the same.

That's the thing with sovereignty. You can have as much of it as you want, but when it comes to selling something, the customer chooses how they want it. And most markets want it to international standards. So sovereignty or not, that's the standard Britain is going to have to reach if it wants to trade. You can get out the EU, but there's always another international system of standard-keeping you have to sign up to. The Codex is just part of a web of international standards bodies.

While Norway is an EU rule taker and not a rule maker, it actually plays quite a canny game. Take the Fish and Fisheries

Product Committee of the Codex Alimentarius. It has 170 officials from the 50 to 60 countries most interested in seafood. It creates the rules accepted by the WTO, which then trickle down to the EU and nation states.

Fishing is a subject the Norwegians feel strongly about. It's a major part of their economy, a lifeline for coastal towns and considered a crucial aspect of the Norwegian character and culture. So it should be unsurprising to find that the chair of the Fish and Fisheries Product Committee of the Codex Alimentarius is a Norwegian: Bjorn Knudtsen. His influential committee sets standards on public safety and fair trading in the world of fish.

Norway is also consulted on the drafting of new laws by the European Commission. Then once the European law is written, civil servants in Oslo work with EU officials to adapt it into Norwegian law.

There is also a 'Right of Reservation', where Norway can refuse to accept an EU law. Norway toyed with this idea once, over the Postal Services Directive, which threatened to open up its postal service to competition. This power is rarely invoked, however, because the EU expressly punishes its use. Once invoked, the affected part of the agreement is suspended, meaning you lose access to that part of the market. But it is there if needed, as a nuclear option.

All in all, it is not a bad package. Norway has to pay in significantly less money than a full EU member. It can influence EU law from above, before it reaches the EU, and below, when the EU passes it down. It has the economic benefits of the single market but only has to implement 21% of all EU law. It is exempt from tranches of law on agriculture, fisheries, justice and home affairs.

Assuming that Britain leaves the customs union, it would still be able to strike its own trade deals – and could probably secure better ones, because it would have the advantage of membership of the single market without the cumbersome ratification process of being in the EU.

For many liberal Brexiters, who dislike the EU but aren't particularly motivated by immigration, the Norway model offers something historic – a chance to wrestle the single market from the control of the EU. They have faith that a British presence in EFTA would fundamentally alter the political centre of gravity on the Continent. A de facto two-speed Europe would be created, perhaps ending in EFTA and the Eurozone sharing the single market, like two anglers in a lake.

Switzerland

On the face of it, Switzerland's special deal with the EU should be attractive. It is utterly bespoke and it is the settled deal of a country whose attitude to the EU is similar to Britain's. Unfortunately, it is also so fiendishly complicated that trying to understand it is like repeatedly slamming your hand in a door. The EU hates it, the Swiss are frankly baffled by it and it leaves the two sides perpetually at loggerheads.

The story of how the Swiss deal came about will be instantly recognisable to a British audience. In 1992, Swiss voters rejected the idea of joining the other EU-objectors in the European Economic Area. The Swiss People's Party, a kind of Alpine UKIP, helped swing the vote by telling a grand story about Swiss culture being diluted and Swiss democracy being outsourced. Mainstream politicians responded by glumly warning about isolationism and the need for a coordinated economic policy – and lost. The Swiss people rejected the single market by 50.3% to 49.7%. This alarmed the Swiss government because the single market made excellent business sense. So it found a way around the vote. It went to the EU with a proposed list of topics to negotiate in exchange for access to the single market.

That negotiation took six years. It came up with multiple agreements. Because of the Swiss obsession with referendums, each would have to be put to the people. But the EU pulled a devious trick. It said Switzerland had to agree the deal in its entirety. If one part was terminated, it all fell apart. No pick-and-mix. High stakes poker. This time the Swiss public agreed the deal. But it was not the same as being in the European Economic Area. It was a series of bilateral treaties.

The lack of wriggle room in the Swiss agreement can be demonstrated by Switzerland's struggle to limit immigration. In 2014, Switzerland narrowly backed a referendum 'against mass immigration' and voted to give priority to Swiss people in law. The EU treated this vote with disdain. Eventually the Swiss government settled for granting local preferences in job hires, but nothing like what was demanded in the referendum.

Essentially the Swiss agreement is a stalemate which fossilised into a status quo. The public is puzzled by the arrangement, allowing the Swiss People's Party to present all political events as an injustice against the cultural purity of the national character. In the European Economic Area, the requirements are similar but at least the system is more readily comprehensible. You are in a club with constantly evolving rules, and if you are unhappy about something there is a court to whom you can complain. The system can be understood by someone without a PhD.

Not so in Switzerland. If there is a change to single market rules a committee of officials from the European Commission and the Swiss government thrash out how to amend an annex in the agreement. It's a laborious, tedious and badly misunderstood process which limits Swiss influence. The arrangement might technically consist of bilateral treaties, but the power relations are heavily weighted in favour of the European Union. In effect, it's unilateral. And it gets more unilateral as time goes by.

Brussels has now started introducing dynamic clauses to new treaties, like Schengen. That means the treaty automatically updates whenever there is a change at EU level. Whatever changes are made in future, Switzerland must automatically accept them. This reduces Switzerland to the status of a standard EEA member. The fact it technically comes through a bilateral deal is immaterial.

Every new Shengen decision goes through the Swiss parliament and each one can lead to a referendum, but the immigration referendum shows how superficial this is. The EU always holds the winning card by saying the whole agreement is null and void if the Swiss reject any part of it. There are several technical safeguards in the relationship, but very few practical ones.

There are some modest advantages to the Swiss. They have a strong sense that smaller countries are better off on their own, taking their own path, and generally accept the arrangement, albeit with a big dollop of resignation. To be fair, for a tiny country of eight million people, Switzerland has held its own as well as could be expected against an international body representing half a billion people. By contrast, the eastern European states that joined later had to swallow almost everything given to them by the EU.

There is little appetite to change things. Certainly, very few people call for Switzerland to join the EU and comparatively few want to break off all ties. So something must be working. And Switzerland remains a prosperous and pleasant place to live.

But the EU hates the Swiss deal. You can imagine why. In an organisation founded on the principle of cooperation through membership, it is extremely finicky and time-consuming. It doesn't fit into any of the EU's storage categories – EEA, customs union, eurozone, nothing. It's a bespoke continental arrangement in a system designed to wipe them out.

The Swiss experience has arguably made the EU even less receptive to British offers than it might have been otherwise. Westminster ministers often talk of wanting to 'carve out' sectors of the economy for membership of the customs union or the single market. But the complexity of the Swiss arrangement means European officials are unlikely to want to replicate it.

Nevertheless, there are some modest reasons to believe Europe might yield a little. Germany has a habit of saying pointedly that Britain cannot secure 'full' single market access without the four freedoms. That suggests that more limited access might be available. There may be room for progress there. But even if the relationship between the UK and Germany is as productive and reasonable as possible, it would not necessarily trump the protests of the EU's 26 other states and nor would it be doable in such a short timeframe.

It is impossible to predict with any confidence whether Britain can salvage any level of single market access from the talks or what form that would take. But unless there is a significant change in the European or British position, it seems likely that the UK will leave the single market.

If anything, positions hardened in the year following the referendum. British ministers kept making factually inaccurate promises to voters about Europe and kept ratcheting up their promises about hard Brexit, either to placate backbenchers or because they really believed them. In response, European leaders grew ever more frustrated by the arrogance exuded by Westminster. It was a deadly process which served to make a successful negotiation even less likely. Feelings towards Britain became even more poisonous when Theresa May claimed that European leaders were trying to subvert the 2017 British general election.

Once again, all this could change as events interrupt and influence the talks. It is perfectly possible that, as the UK economy deteriorates, the government will sharply alter course. But the current direction of travel is clear and it points to a hard Brexit outside the single market.

Diagram 4

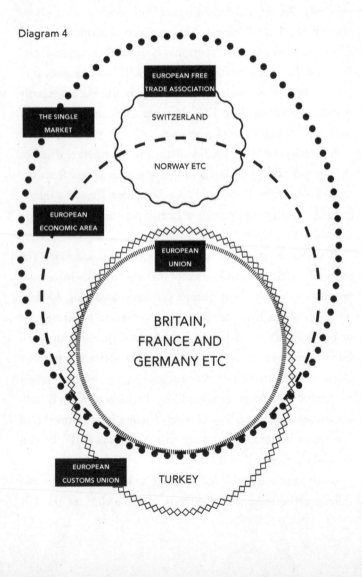

Turkey

There is a chance Britain could leave the single market and stay in the customs union. As we saw earlier, the European single market allows the free movement of four things:

- **Goods**
- **Capital**
- **Services**
- **People**

A customs union is only about the taxation of goods. It allows goods to be moved between its members without paying tariffs and has one common tariff arrangement for goods coming from outside. So you can export, say, pasta from Italy to France without paying any tariffs at the French border. But if you wanted to ship pasta from the United States to France, or any other EU state, you would have to pay a tariff and the same tariff regardless of which EU state you were entering.

Currently, only one major country is outside of the EU and inside the European Customs Union: Turkey (see Diagram 4, left). Its case is very different to Britain. When Turkey joined the customs union it was a stepping stone to full EU membership – the latest chapter in Turkey's historic journey towards the West. Since then a growing European nativism and the rule of hardline president Recep Tayyip Erdoğan have put paid to those dreams.

There are some advantages to being in the customs union even if, like Turkey, you are outside the single market. It removes tariffs in trade with Europe and allows you to enjoy some of the benefits of any deals negotiated with outside countries by the

European Commission's very experienced negotiating team, which is arguably the best in the world.

Nevertheless, the chances of Britain remaining in the customs union are slim: the creation of a Department for International Trade seemed to be something of a give-away about the direction of travel.

There is a reason for that, which owes more to politics than economics. Remaining in the customs union would make ministers' lives more difficult. They urgently need a sunny upland with which to counter all the doom and gloom being doled out by journalists about the perils of Brexit. They are currently able to do this by pointing to the trade deals Britain will be able to negotiate with major economies once it is free of the dead hand of Brussels. This is far more problematic than they make out, but staying in the customs union would deprive them even of that meagre political currency.

The business costs of this piece of political decision-making are very high. Raoul Ruparel, who was hired by David Davis to provide expertise on the Brexit process, has admitted that leaving the customs union would reduce GDP by between 1 and 1.2% in the long term and cost the UK economy £25 billion a year. Other studies expect the hit to GDP to reach 4.5% by 2030. This is because leaving the customs union opens a Pandora's Box of bureaucratic horror, as we saw in the introduction.

The first thing businesses exporting to the EU will have to do is to provide information about their product in order to establish its classification code. That code then allows them to ascertain the tariff and work out their export processing costs.

This is not a simple process. Take biscuits. Biscuits come under the designation of 'composite agrigoods'. These are established by the percentages of milk fat, milk proteins, starch or glucose or various forms of sugar in the product. To calculate the final rate you have to cross reference 504 potential recipes to 27 kinds of product, leaving 13,608 categories of bakery or confectionery goods, all with potentially different export rate duties.

At the border, customs officials will stop the goods and check the classification, along with background information on the product. With salmon, they will ask: is it frozen? Is it wild or farmed? Because tariffs are calculated on cost, they must then assess the stated price of the item and decide whether the correct amount of customs duty has been paid.

Then the real nightmare begins: country of origin checks, which assess not only the country the good has come from, but also where its components parts come from. These checks are despairingly complicated. The key issue is whether the EU has preferential trade agreements with third countries who have made a component. Take cars. Cars often have parts from all over the world. If a car has lots of parts from Mexico and Mexico does not have a trade agreement with the EU, the vehicle may be blocked from entering the customs union or charged additional duty.

So a business sending its products into the customs union is likely to have to establish where every single component originates. For products which are built using an international construction chain, this can be a Herculean task.

The certification for a specific item lasts for three years, but that's not much use to a manufacturer whose products keep changing. For many businesses this bureaucratic requirement is more damaging to their day-to-day operations than a tariff. Usually, a tariff cost can be absorbed. But the inconvenience of country of origins checks are a perpetual and costly obstacle to trade.

There is another final aspect to the customs union which will bring back gloomy memories for middle aged Britons. Leaving it will transport holidaymakers back to the days of excise duties, and a return to limits on how many bottles of spirits and packs of cigarettes can be brought back to the UK.

As with all aspects of Brexit, these effects can be mitigated. Countries in the European Economic Area, for instance, have a special regime which reduces this burden. But to obtain such an opt-out requires time and patient negotiation. And as we have seen, they are in short supply.

Canada

Leaving the single market and the customs union means that the closest economic relationship the UK and Europe can expect to have is a free trade deal, like the one recently negotiated between the EU and Canada. Securing one would allow Britain to trade with the EU while reducing tariffs, country of origin checks and non-tariff barriers. In practical terms this is probably what ministers have in mind when they speak about access to the single market.

Modern free trade agreements are vast and complicated, covering all sorts of diverse and highly technical matters, including conformity assessments for products, intellectual property rights and technical regulation. So British ministers would do well to remember two things. The first is that negotiating a new trade deal will take years — far longer than just the two years provided by Article 50, even if there is a short transition period attached to it. The second is that one may never be signed at all.

Trade deals have fallen out of fashion. Their complexity and growing public wariness mean there hasn't been a major world one for a quarter of a century. The last was the Uruguay Round of the WTO in 1993. The Doha Round started in 2001 and was abandoned in 2015 after disagreements over agriculture, industrial tariffs, non-tariff barriers and various other matters. Once Trump became US President he started trying to tear up the North American Trade Agreement (NAFTA).

Bilateral deals are considered the new alternative to massive agreements, but they are also struggling. A US-EU trade deal, the Transatlantic Trade and Investment Partnership, included a secretive investor dispute mechanism which would let private companies take national governments to a specialised court if they felt their interests had been contradicted by political decisions. Left wing activists smelled a rat. Protests started in Paris and Berlin may have scuppered the deal altogether. However, Brexit appeared to startle the EU, which redoubled its efforts to finalise a trade deal with Japan and managed to ratify its deal with Canada.

Yet even here, the process has been incredibly time consuming. Negotiations with Canada started in 2009. The treaty was only signed in 2016 after a tortuous progression through all the national parliaments of the EU. In Belgium, that process involved securing the approval of regional parliaments, including in French-speaking Wallonia. Here it ran into problems, with leftist leaders saying they would veto it due to the powers it gave multinational corporations. After a tense few days in which the Canadians appeared to give up any hope of getting the deal agreed, it finally scraped through; but it was touch and go.

This is the reality of trade deals. Once they go out to national parliaments, they are vulnerable to the whims of every lobby group on the Continent. Anyone from a Hungarian widget manufacturer to a French pyjama maker can lobby their government to reject the deal. Things get bogged down in domestic politics.

A British deal has one significant advantage over a Canadian one – as an existing single market member, the UK already has regulatory equivalence. However, it also has several disadvantages. Firstly, it needs to set up an agency supervising compliance with the European market and have it recognised by the Commission. That may sound relatively straightforward but it is easier said than done. There are very few people in the Commission who can do this and they generally take their time. In the white heat of a time-sensitive trade deal, it is another process not controlled by Britain.

More importantly, a UK deal would be heavily reliant on services because of their prominence in the economy. These played a much smaller role in the Canadian deal. Services are much more complicated than goods. Getting a package of eggs over a border just involves producing and packaging them to the right standard. Getting a customer in the UK to accept a Slovakian solicitor is another matter entirely. There are big cultural and practical difficulties to securing regulatory equivalence for a service.

And of all the services, financial services are the most complex. It's a highly volatile area where European countries will fight to protect their own sectors from the might of the City. They may also have strategic reasons for adopting a harsh negotiating position. After all, the less business goes to London, the more goes to Berlin, Frankfurt and Paris. A trade deal provides an opportunity for the EU to grab business and market share, which the Canadian deal did not.

The Canadian deal also had the advantage of being politics-free. The British deal most emphatically does not. It will take place when feelings are running high. Its provisions will be seen by European leaders through the prism of their domestic audience. And one of the primary motivations in Brussels will be to protect the union against a potentially destabilising deal.

One thing is clear: it cannot be done in two years. Even if Britain had an army of trade experts and negotiators, which it does not, a detailed deal is inconceivable in such a short time frame.

The UK will have to either extend Article 50 or put in place interim arrangements to cover the period between the end of talks and the ratification of a deal with the EU. Otherwise it will face the cliff edge of trade havoc and a severe economic shock.

The World Trade Organisation

Once Britain is out the EU, it is on World Trade Organisation rules. Brexit supporters have long claimed that the WTO is a safety net for the UK, a safe place for it to land once it finally leaves Europe. They portray the WTO as a virile, regulation-free wonderland just waiting for Britain to take its place as one of the world's leading trading nations.

It is nothing of the sort. The WTO is a potential regulatory nightmare, where each and every member can trigger a trade dispute against you. To join it, Britain must conduct some of the most technical, complicated, unprecedented trade negotiations in political history.

Furthermore, the WTO is not some place you escape to if your deal with the EU goes wrong. The WTO will only work for Britain if it is co-operating effectively with the EU. A decent EU negotiation is a precondition of successful WTO membership.

Leading Brexiters say the EU and UK can unilaterally reduce their tariffs with each other and then go to the WTO as tariff-free entities. But the only way in which this arrangement would be legal under WTO rules is if the UK and the EU have signed a trade deal first. If they have not signed a trade deal, they are barred from unilaterally lowering their tariffs with one another.

Setting new trade rules

The WTO has a rule called 'most favoured nation'. It's a very unhelpful name, because it entails the opposite of what it implies. It means that you cannot discriminate in your tariffs. If, say, you want to drop your tariffs on beef to zero with the EU, you must drop them to zero with everyone.

So Britain could unilaterally drop its EU tariffs, but then it would become a completely tariff-free country. Cheap foreign goods would flood the market and hundreds of thousands of people would lose their jobs. It would also make the UK a less attractive country for trade deals, because its tariffs would already be non-existent. It would be like offering your product for free when a customer is prepared to pay.

The EU must apply external tariffs to Britain if it leaves without a trade deal. It doesn't matter what the German car industry or anyone else wants. It's not a question of being vindictive. If it ignored the 'most favoured nation' rule the EU would be deluged by successful disputes and have to offer massive trade compensation or face retaliation against its exports to other states.

The UK could opt for the stick, rather than the carrot, and threaten the EU with higher tariffs unless a trade deal is done before Brexit talks are concluded, but this would hit Britain harder than the EU. Britain would have to raise tariffs for all other countries, starving it of imports and starting its new life as an independent trading nation in the worst imaginable way.

Instead, Britain will have to focus on establishing itself independently inside the WTO. This is not as easy as it sounds. There are no rules for what happens at this point. They simply do not exist.

There are WTO rules on becoming a member, but they are irrelevant because Britain is already a member. Some Remainers and a few lawyers maintain that the UK needs to become a member, but the WTO's director general Roberto Azevedo clarified: 'The UK is a member of the WTO today, it will continue to be a member tomorrow.'

That is pretty much where the good news ends. From then on things get seriously murky. Members of the WTO have things called 'schedules' – one on goods and one on services. These are lists of commitments to other countries, laying out your tariffs and subsidies. They define the terms upon which you trade with other states.

They are very long, complicated and boring. A typical schedule lays out things like what percentage share of your local banks foreign banks are allowed to buy, what kinds of financial instruments can be bought and sold, whether your insurance companies can operate health insurance, the tariff rate on textiles, clothing, cars and flowers etc. It is no less than a full description of how you deal economically with the rest of the world.

Britain is now trying to extract its schedules from the EU's. This is an incredibly arduous and labour-intensive puzzle. The WTO has rules for modifying schedules, but not for extracting them from a customs union. This is uncharted water. The reason it is uncharted is because no-one has ever been crazy enough to try it before.

Unlike the EU, the WTO isn't based on a notion of formal hierarchy. It prefers to get things done by providing a forum for discussion. That sounds very nice, but in practice it means that each and every member state can object to any number of issues. Maybe all the other countries on earth will accept the process Britain proposes for extracting its schedules. Maybe they will not. It is possible the WTO secretariat will have to step in and set up a process. Or perhaps a neutral state will do it.

But if even one of the WTO's other 163 members, which includes all the EU member states and also the EU itself as a separate entity, object to any part of what we do, things get complicated. This process can be either nightmarish or tolerable. The distinction between these positions relies on the skill of the UK negotiations.

Fortunately, people want to trade with one another, particularly when it's a country like Britain with a strong consumer base. And unlike at Brussels, Britain currently enjoys goodwill at the WTO, which it helped to set up. It's seen as a respectable trading nation, which is instinctively averse to protectionism and abides by its global commitments (though Brexit is damaging that reputation).

But even then, ministers should not be under any illusions about sentimentality, even from the likes of the US or Australia. The UK is dealing with professional trade negotiators. These people squeeze you. It's what they do. Trade negotiations are not the place for a group hug. States go into them with a very firm focus on their interests and they take advantage of vulnerability to increase their market access and create opportunities for domestic industries.

Usually aspiring member states wrap up all their issues before they join the WTO, but Britain's strange situation means it can probably start trading provisionally on the basis of the schedules it puts down while dealing with any disputes over them. What this means is that the UK will form its own calculations about its share of the EU's tariffs and subsidies and start trading on that basis. Any countries which object can then go into negotiations. But while those discussions are held, trade can continue on the basis of what has been proposed.

Is this legal? No-one knows really, but it's hard to envisage anyone causing too much of a stir. If they did, Britain might be able to rely on the continuity principle of international law

– which does exactly what it says on the tin. Again it is unclear how well this would work. At this point everything is novel.

In a sense, this seems a much more advantageous situation than Britain had at the EU. There are looser rules on talks and the UK does not face a cliff edge at which point the economic consequences become severe. But that would not be a useful way of looking at the system. The variables in the WTO system are alarming. It is like quicksand. Once you get dragged into one dispute, a host of others can open up, leaving you gasping for breath and at the mercy of countless predatory trading partners.

Britain is going to have to get its schedules clear with all the member states in the WTO – big or small, rich or poor, friendly or unfriendly. And it will be doing so at a moment of profound vulnerability.

National opportunism

Hostile nations will be watching carefully. Russia will find ample opportunity to make life difficult. China, as we will see, has strategic reasons to make the process tumultuous. Countries embroiled in territorial disputes with the UK will see an opportunity to advance their agenda. Spain might see it as an opportunity to move towards securing joint-sovereignty over Gibraltar. Argentina might use it as a chance to progress its claim on the Falklands. Neither of these issues have anything to do with what's going on at the WTO, but this unusual situation gives them leverage. Trade talks can easily become an opportunity for countries to advance unrelated agendas.

Britain is not even at the head of the queue in this process. The EU is in the same situation. It needs to have the WTO approve its new schedules once Britain's have been extracted from them. Because it is much larger, the EU is likely to get priority. And if the break-up talks end acrimoniously, it could be a hostile actor.

Once again, ministers' approach to the talks is crucial. If they had a moderately good-tempered Article 50 negotiation and left with an EU trade deal in hand, things would look pretty good. There hopefully wouldn't be any tariffs and ideally there would be mutual recognition agreements with the EU and maybe even the states they hold them with, like the US. The other members of the WTO would know the degree of Britain's access to the single market. A cancerous growth of uncertainty would have been surgically removed from the process.

If there is no trade deal, everything becomes more complicated. Britain can expect the EU and member states to raise objections to the schedules it puts down. Affected third parties are likely to raise objections too – either because the new schedules disadvantage them or because Brexit presents an opportunity to maximise their exports.

The potential for getting bogged down in decades of trade disputes – and even potentially risking a full-on trade war – is significant. Britain will have to tread very carefully.

External Tariffs

The first task is to simplify the process. That means replicating all the EU's external tariffs. The EU has 10% on cars, so the UK will have 10% on cars. Britain has to replicate everything. Even tinkering with this system would trigger an avalanche of complaints which the government is no position to deal with.

Of course, this automatically discredits the entire argument for Brexit. Britain would not really control its tariffs until some distant point in the future, if at all. The only way to survive the transition from WTO membership under the EU to WTO membership outside the EU is to keep things exactly as they were when Britain was in the EU. The sovereignty over tariffs and all sorts of other matters secured by Brexit is frittered away at the WTO, simply to ensure stability.

This is less than ideal for UK interests. It means it will continue to be the servant of a system which was designed for a group of countries to which it no longer belongs. The EU tariffs are built around EU interests. They are protectionist in some areas Britain would not want them to be and insufficiently protectionist in areas where it might wish them to be. Brussels has special rules for oranges, for example, which wouldn't be at the top of a British government's list of priorities, because they are not grown in the UK. It abided by that system as an EU member on the assumption that Brussels would fight for its national interests in other areas which did affect it. But to give up on membership and then keep the same tariffs is the worst of all worlds. Nevertheless, this is what Britain must do.

It will do so despite coming under deep and widespread pressure by industry to do otherwise. Countless lobbying groups will urge the UK to make big changes, and in many cases they will be entirely right to do so.

Take the British sugar company Tate & Lyle. It does not like the EU tariffs.

Sugar can be refined in two ways. There's beet, a root crop grown in Europe – especially in France, but in the UK too. And then there's cane, a giant grass which grows in tropical parts of the world. As a legacy of colonialism, Tate and Lyle depends on sugar cane for production. But the EU doesn't much care about cane, for the rather predictable reason that there isn't any in its territory. So it protects beet and not cane. Westminster will have one part of the British sugar industry demanding one thing and the other part demanding something else entirely.

There are areas of policy like this all over the place, esoteric bits of the economy that ordinary people have never heard of but which relevant industries care about very much. As soon as this process starts, the government will be besieged by groups trying to improve their situation.

But if the government responds to industrial requests and raises a tariff in one area, it has to drop one somewhere else. That's how the WTO works. It's not about money. It is a commercial contract based on reciprocal concessions. It's about trading degrees of market access. If you protect an industry over here, you must reduce protections for another industry over there.

Who will that upset? Which sector will lose out? What if they lose out so badly that they have to lay off workers? How prominent will the photos of those workers be on the front pages? How strongly will they lobby the government for a change? How many political battles can the government fight at once? Once it starts modifying EU tariffs, the dominoes would fall everywhere, in a nightmarish wave of lobbying and technical adjustments. The only way to avoid this is to leave the EU tariffs in place.

Things get more difficult when it comes to another element of the global trading system, tariff rate quotas, because here Britain can't replicate the EU figures.

Import quotas

Tariff rate quotas specify that a particular kind of product has a certain tariff up to a set level of imports, and then another tariff once you go over that amount. So for instance the first 100,000 tonnes of wheat you import might be at 2%, and anything above that at 10%.

The trouble is that the quotas are calculated across the whole of the EU. So what should the quota be just for Britain? It's not easy to work out.

Take chicken. The EU imports a lot of processed chicken from Brazil and Thailand. Brazil exports about 480,000 tonnes to the EU, of which about 40,000 goes to the UK. Thailand sends 240,000 tonnes to the EU and about half of that goes to the UK.

Britain is now trying to designate the imports according to however much it received over the last three years. But regardless of whether that is fair or not, Brazil and Thailand now have an opportunity. Their poultry industry will be lobbying their governments to prise open the UK market a little more. After all, it is a strong market for them and they are suddenly in a position of relative strength. But if the UK goes along with that and increases its quota level, it will face angry protests from British chicken farmers.

The quota issue is one of the most dreadful types of problems: technical, fiendishly complicated, with many potential opponents, and taking place at a moment of acute political and economic crisis when most of your resources are directed elsewhere.

Subsidies

There's a similar problem with subsidies, which are worked out on the basis of aggregate levels of support across the EU. This is politically explosive. The moment Britain drops its subsidies for farming, many farms will go bust and the countryside will change beyond recognition. And it's not just in the UK that the debate is so crucial. Agricultural subsidies are a flash point across the WTO. The world will be watching very closely.

Britain faces other problems protecting its domestic industries from the global markets. It will urgently want to maintain EU arrangements against the dumping of Chinese steel. The moment the UK is not included, the steel industry in Wales and the north of England would face collapse as cheap Chinese steel floods the market. But if it tries to maintain the EU protections, the Chinese will object and demand a new UK investigation demonstrating domestic injury and unfair trade. Until that dispute is resolved, Beijing will challenge any new trade remedy. This dispute, which will be almost impossible to avoid, will rumble on for years.

As things stand, Britain cannot even fight back in that dispute because it does not have an authority to undertake trade remedy investigations. It can set one up, but again, the same problem comes up: too much to do, with too little time and too few trade experts.

Even with all the right infrastructure and diplomacy at the WTO level during Article 50 negotiations, the UK is bound to be sucked into some disputes. For each one, there will be a series of consultations lasting a month or two. If that doesn't work, it will go in front of a settlement panel for a ruling. A loss can be appealed, but that's the end of the line. A WTO member state which does not comply with a ruling is subject to sanctions. That's rare. There's a 90% compliance rate at the panel. But given the UK's legal weakness, it could easily lose many cases and either see sanctions mount or be forced to trade under conditions imposed by other countries.

The UK also needs to join the government procurement agreement, which allows companies to compete for contracts on certain types of government projects over 10 million euros. It's backed up by a dispute resolution mechanism. The EU signed this and the UK was included by default. Is the UK still a member? No-one knows. If this system stops, Britain's domestic firms won't be able to bid for contracts in the US or elsewhere. This is not a small matter: government procurement is a big money-spinner for UK firms.

Similar changes could affect specialist producers. Firms making regional specialities will be concerned about any move away from the EU's geographical indication system. These are the rules that say that you can only call something champagne if it comes from the Champagne region of France, or parmesan if it comes from five specific areas of northern Italy.

The Americans are not fans. They prefer trademarks to geographical indicators. But Britain has plenty of companies which benefit from this system, including West Country farmhouse cheddar, stilton cheese, Welsh lamb, cumberland sausages, watercress and Cornish pasties. These producers will struggle to maintain that recognition outside the EU.

When you put that nightmarish combination of negotiations together, Britain is facing as hard a task at the WTO as it is at the EU.

Britain is facing protracted negotiations, requiring governing bodies which it does not currently have, at precisely the moment when it is most vulnerable due to a sudden change in its tariff and non-tariff arrangements with Europe. At best the WTO option is survivable. But under no circumstances is it desirable.

How can we keep the UK together?

Most of Britain's difficulties are based on its desire to maintain the financial benefits of the European Union while extracting itself from sharing any sovereignty. But there is an aspect to the British dilemma outside that trade-off: keeping the United Kingdom together. Scotland and Northern Ireland voted by 62% and 55% respectively to stay in the EU. It is unclear whether the UK's current constitutional arrangements can survive contact with the EU machine.

Scotland

On the morning of 24 June, when David Cameron was resigning and Boris Johnson and Michael Gove looked shocked to discover that they might be in charge, Scotland's first minister Nicola Sturgeon looked like one of the few political leaders in Britain to have any composure.

Brexit felt like it might be a definitive chapter in the story of how Scotland left the UK. The socio-political chasm between the two countries had never seemed bigger. And worst of all, Guy Verhofstadt at the European Parliament soon started making promising noises about Scottish membership of the EU. But the undercurrents have not been as positive for independence as members of the Scottish National Party might have thought. Nicola Sturgeon is in a tough position.

For a start, the polling is unhelpful. The number of people who said they would vote for independence in a second referendum following the Brexit vote is largely unchanged from the 44% who voted for independence in 2014.

Asking Scottish voters to choose between the European single market and the British single market is also fraught with risk: the British single market is worth four times as much in terms of jobs and trade. Westminster also helps plug the gap in Scotland's £15 billion annual deficit. The EU isn't directly transferring funds of anything like that magnitude. Looking at figures like that, it's hard to imagine an electorate making a different choice to the one they made last time. Even politically, the debate over Brexit is not as clear as Sturgeon's rhetoric would imply. Around half a million SNP voters also voted to get out of the EU.

Sturgeon faces bad polling on one side and terrible economic arguments on the other. But in the aftermath of the EU referendum she came under pressure to call a second vote on independence, especially since she could argue that one was warranted by a material change in Scotland's circumstances. Many of the new, single-minded supporters who joined the SNP after the first independence referendum wanted Sturgeon to get on with things. She needed to offer constant signs of progress to keep them in line, but without making the sort of firm commitment which would trigger a referendum.

As part of this tricky balancing act, Scotland's First Minister overreached. In the days after the vote, she ended up saying that a second referendum was highly likely. 'It is a significant material change in circumstances,' she said. 'It's a statement of the obvious that the option of a second independence referendum must be on the table, and it is on the table.'

Months later she started consultations on a bill for a second vote and shortly after that began to establish the legal basis upon which it could take place. These moves were probably intended more as a sign of progress and to give her maximum room to manoeuvre, but soon enough she was forced to confirm that she did plan to hold another referendum. In the June 2017 general election this promise proved toxic to many voters in Scotland and the SNP lost seats to the Conservatives.

This might make it seem as if Downing Street had strategically outplayed Sturgeon but dig beneath the day to day party politics and things aren't quite that simple.

Theresa May began her premiership with a visit to Scotland and Northern Ireland, promising that agreement from both governments would form a central part of the Brexit negotiation package. At this stage, Downing Street could have made plenty of offers to Sturgeon.

The first involved a previously little-noticed advantage of Brexit for the devolved assemblies. Agriculture and fisheries, which were always devolved matters, had until this point been under the control of the European Union. So while Scotland could technically do what it liked in this area, in practice it and the UK both had the same policy, which was whatever the EU said it should be. With the EU cord cut, Scotland would regain control of a large new policy brief.

Potentially this was a problem for Westminster, because it would allow Scotland to create very different standards for agriculture, the environment, and food. However, London could have tried to block this by making the argument that the devolution agreement was made on the assumption that Scotland and the rest of the UK would remain part of the EU, and if they were not, those devolution rights would not hold.

Or Downing Street could have offered the carrot instead of the stick, by promising not to interfere with these policy areas as they transferred to Holyrood. Instead Theresa May dangled the possibility of allowing Scottish control without providing any detail of how she might do so. The Scottish government was left feeling suspicious and resentful.

There were other tactics available. The repeal bill, converting EU law into British law, which we'll come to later, is one of the most powerful pieces of legislation proposed by Westminster in decades. London could have offered Sturgeon a role in defining Holyrood's role in that, granting Scotland a high degree of autonomy in what would be a very wide-ranging legislative change. Instead, the small print of the bill only allowed Scottish politicians to grapple with EU law if it fitted into Westminster's existing strategy.

Generous offers in these areas, combined with a consensual approach which paid due respect to the Scottish vote, could have given Sturgeon the space to do what the polls and the economic data suggested she do anyway: refrain from holding a second referendum. She would have to explain why she was not holding a vote, but at least the first minister would be able to brandish a significant transfer of power from London to Scotland to keep supporters in line.

Downing Street did not bother pursuing any of these angles. Ministers did not discuss the devolved aspects of the EU's remit with their counterparts in Scotland. They did not make any offers on the repeal bill. Instead, May went to the Conservative party conference and all but confirmed the most extreme interpretation of the Brexit vote. She did not mention the fact that the vote was tight, nor that Scotland had voted to Remain. Ministers then announced a series of policies – from 'naming and shaming' companies which employed foreign workers, to locking up estate agents who did not check their tenants immigration papers – which further alienated the progressive SNP. Sturgeon was reduced to tweeting out her objections. Relations never recovered from this early expression of disrespect.

Instead of trying to establish a new consensus in post-Brexit Britain between England and Scotland, May's actions seemed to corroborate the SNP argument that Westminster is at best indifferent about, and at worst openly hostile to, Scotland. For the time being the SNP have been electorally knocked back, but if that sense of arrogance combines with an increasingly bleak financial picture as a result of Brexit, it could prove a heady mix for the nationalists. It may eventually be enough to outweigh the economic arguments against an independent Scotland and fatigue with SNP government.

Of all the problems Downing Street faces, the Scottish one is the least immediate. But it is certain that Westminster's initial behaviour after the referendum result has made it more likely that Brexit might eventually tear apart the United Kingdom.

Ireland

The problems in Scotland look like pleasantries next to those in Ireland. At stake is nothing less than a reversal of two decades of careful progress since the Troubles. And yet government ministers have seemed largely uninterested in the impact of Brexit across the Irish Sea.

At the heart of that confusion has been a failure, once again, to understand how the EU operates. Ministers would often state that they wanted the Republic of Ireland to refrain from certain acts, such as imposing a hard border on Northern Ireland, seemingly without realising that they were not in the Republic's gift. As an EU member the Republic is bound to follow the EU's rules. The place to lobby was Brussels, but once again ministers underestimated the complexity of the negotiating problem and misunderstood how and where the EU makes decisions.

At one point the Brexit minister David Davis even gave an interview in which he suggested the Republic of Ireland was part of the UK. He told Sky's *Murnaghan* programme 'one of our really challenging issues... will be the internal border we have with southern Ireland'. At first it appeared to be a slip of the tongue, but then he repeated it: 'We are not going to go about creating other internal borders inside the United Kingdom'.

In reality, the border in Ireland is the UK's only external land border. It is also its only land border with the EU and one of the key pressure points in the UK/EU relationship. Outside of Calais, it will be the main location at which the implications of Brexit on trade are felt. As things currently stand, it is very soft indeed. People cross it, often several times a day, as do goods and services, without checks. But if Britain leaves the customs union, checks for country of origin rules would have to take place. And if the UK leaves the single market, things become yet more complicated. Products crossing the border would not necessarily comply with single market rules, so some would need to be detained and tested.

It's not just goods. The qualifications of people on one side of the border might not be recognised on the other side. Suddenly an accountant who works in one part of Ireland but who qualified in another might find that he has to return to where he first got his certificate. The pensions of people on one side of the border may not be guaranteed on the other.

But the real fear in Ireland is the return of a hard border for people. This would end the free travel area established by the UK and the Republic of Ireland when the free state was established in 1922. It is hard to predict the political consequences of re-establishing a hard border for people in Ireland, but it is likely that supporters of Irish reunification would view it as worsening of the practical implications of partition. It could very well pose a threat to the peace process. The post-election pact between the Conservatives and the DUP has only raised questions about Westminster's ability to act as a neutral arbiter in Northern Ireland.

After Britain leaves the EU, the most obvious danger is that the EU would ask the Republic of Ireland to join the Schengen free travel area, which relies on strong external border controls so that it can maintain passport-free travel inside. This is unlikely, but even if it did occur, Britain and Ireland have considerable legal protection. Three protocols annexed to the Treaty on the Functioning of the EU are pertinent: Protocol 19, which states that Britain and the Republic are not automatically covered by Schengen rules or by proposals to develop them; Protocol 20, which allows the UK and Republic of Ireland to 'continue to make arrangements between themselves relating to the movement of persons between their territories'; and Protocol 21, which allows the UK and the Republic of Ireland to opt in to immigration or asylum legislation other than Schengen rules.

As it happens, Europe has long recognised the unique difficulties of the Irish arrangement and has no more interest in seeing a return to them than the UK or the Republic does. The UK's difficulty is that the specific dynamic of Brexit, including its emphasis on immigration control, pushes it towards the establishment of a hard border for people. If anyone is responsible for the return of a hard border in Ireland, it will be Britain. Years after Brexit, it is easy to imagine a tabloid scare campaign about Polish plumbers using free movement to get to Ireland, then crossing the border and arriving in the UK.

It will be nonsense. Britain will presumably allow Polish people to come over for their holidays either visa free or with a tourism visa, and this route is just as open to abuse as keeping an open border in Ireland. But reason and rationality do not necessarily figure in tabloid campaigns and the momentum against free movement is strong enough that this could easily become a problem in the years ahead, especially if the development of customs controls is already setting up the infrastructure for a hard border on the ground.

For voters in Northern Ireland, the situation is vexing. They warned during the referendum that Brexit would result in this and the truth is that voters, newspapers and political leaders in England simply did not care. The warnings were made and they were ignored. It is not something that will be forgotten quickly.

What are we going to do?

In each and every one of the key issues – freedom of movement, the economy, and preservation of the United Kingdom – the EU machine chews up British demands, mangles them and spits them out. Ending freedom of movement risks the economy and endangers the preservation of the UK. Britain's Brexit ministers have set themselves an impossible task; one whose own internal contradictions make it almost impossible to envisage a tolerable outcome. So what will the Brexit team do?

It is unwise to make political predictions. The variables are too numerous, especially when it comes to Brexit: a problem with countless actors, millions of trade implications, numerous political agendas and a volatile, emotional debate. But we can ask the following questions: what do the leading Brexiters want, how talented are they, what tools do they have at their disposal and in which context do they operate? The answer to those questions grounds our expectations.

What do they want?

Since the Brexit referendum and the June 2017 general election British politics has been volatile and unpredictable, so it's impossible to know if the Brexit ministers in place (Boris Johnson, David Davis, Liam Fox) at the time of writing, October 2017, will still be there by the time you read this. However the behaviour of these men during the referendum campaign and afterwards displayed their ignorance and set the tone of the European response. They have demonstrated a persistent inability to deal realistically with the challenges they face or set out a deliverable goal for the project. Any future British ministerial team will have to work with the confusion and ill-will that they have sown.

The key question facing the 'Three Musketeers' was always what took precedence: following EU rules, including free movement, or staying in the single market? It was almost impossible to ascertain where they stood on this choice, or even if they recognised that it was a choice. How they behaved then lowered Britain's credibility in Brussels and around the world.

In a *Telegraph* column days after the vote, Johnson wrote: 'British people will still be able to go and work in the EU. To live; to travel; to study; to buy homes and to settle down.' He was describing freedom of movement. This would imply Britain was staying in the single market.

In his next *Telegraph* column, Johnson promised the exact opposite: Britain would end freedom of movement and strike a free trade deal with the EU, both of which would only be possible if we left the single market. It was unclear at this stage whether Johnson did not understand the difference between the two positions he had supported, or was simply trying to position himself to benefit from the swirling, unpredictable politics of the post-referendum period.

He then changed tack again and suggested the question simply didn't exist. It was 'absolute baloney' that there was a trade-off between freedom of movement and single market membership. European Parliament president Martin Schulz replied that maintaining single market access without free movement 'is for sure not feasible'. Johnson maintained this distinction was false.

For his part, in one of his first statements to the Commons as Brexit Secretary, David Davis seemed to suggest that controlling immigration was non-negotiable. In a reply to an MP bringing up the single market, he said: 'We don't need to be a member... The simple truth is that if a requirement of membership is giving up control of our borders, I think that makes it very improbable.'

Had Davis given away the prime minister's private view, or was he trying to push her into adopting a more radical position? The prime minister's spokeswoman contorted herself trying to pass off the comments as a personal opinion, despite coming from the minister in charge of implementing the policy he was speaking about.

Perhaps this was because the official position was unclear. For months all Theresa May offered was the meaningless tautology 'Brexit means Brexit'. When she finally offered the public a little more clarity she said: 'What the vote, what leaving the European Union does enable us to do is, yes, to say what I think the British people are very clear about, which is that they don't want free movement to continue in the way that it has done in the past.'

What was interesting about this statement was the phrase 'in the way that it has done'. This was placed at the end of every statement she made about free movement, and that of her ministers. It provided wriggle room for the sorts of deals we outlined earlier, should the Europeans choose to make them. As long as she kept saying that, the door was still open to emergency brakes and job-offer conditions and the like.

But then something changed. When the prime minister took to the stage of the 2016 Conservative party conference in Birmingham, the language was more radical than what we had heard before.

'Let me be clear,' she said. 'We are not leaving the European Union only to give up control of immigration again.' This time there were no caveats. Then she made her comments on the European Court of Justice and food packaging which indicated that she intended to pursue a hard form of Brexit by leaving the single market and the customs union. It was a vision not just of border control, but of total national sovereignty over every aspect of policy.

A few days later David Davis told the Commons: 'We will return sovereignty to the institutions of this United Kingdom. That is what people voted for on 23 June: for Britain to take control of its own destiny, and for all decisions about taxpayers' money, borders and laws to be taken here in Britain.'

But this was not simply a plan for WTO rules. It was clear that Davis wanted to secure a trade agreement with the EU *before* leaving. In response to a question from Tory backbencher

John Redwood on tariffs, he replied: 'It is not just tariff barri-ers. We also have to negotiate non-tariff barriers. It is… in both Europe's interest and our interest to have tariff-free and non-tariff barrier based trade. That is where the jobs are.'

Two days later, the prime minister said: 'What we are going to do is be ambitious in our negotiations to negotiate the best deal for the British people – and that will include the maximum possible access to the European market for firms to trade with and operate within the European market.' Finally, there was a join-the-dots picture: the Government's Brexit plan was to leave the single market and the customs union but somehow try to negotiate a comprehensive free trade agreement within the two-year Article 50 window. It wasn't until January 2017, however, during her speech at Lancaster House, that May explicitly said Britain would be leaving the single market and the customs union.

Before that there had been nearly half a year of coded state-ments and incompatible promises. In fact, the government often pretended specific terms did not even exist. Davis preferred to speak about a 'spectrum of outcomes' rather than single market membership. Johnson said the term single market was 'increasingly useless'. And May said there was no such thing as a choice between 'soft Brexit' and 'hard Brexit' when there most demonstrably was.

In September 2017, over a year after becoming prime minis-ter, May finally accepted what her critics had been saying for months and asked Europe for a two-year transition period, to give extra time for negotiation and avoid the cliff edge outlined in the first chapter of this book. But even as she adopted a more realistic approach to talks, she was still unable to offer a coherent view of what Britain wanted from Brexit.

Even outside the single market, Britain can decide to unilaterally accept EU rules in a bid to facilitate trade. This would not 'take back control', of course. If anything it would lose control, because it would now be governed by regulations it no longer had any role in formulating. But it would reduce the economic impact of Brexit on the UK. Alternately, Britain could diverge from EU regulations. This would certainly take back control, but at a heavy economic price.

There is still, at the time of writing, no clear government position on which of these paths the country should take, or any vision of what a post-Brexit Britain would look like. It is therefore impossible for either the British or European negotiating team to know what is required of them in trade talks.

How talented are they?

The challenges before the Brexit ministerial team were considerable. They had to devise a viable negotiation strategy against a much stronger partner, made up of 27 individual actors operating both independently and in unison, with many ways of blocking progress, to a tight timeframe, in which the smaller partner would always be more disadvantaged if the talks failed. At stake was the economic future of the UK. The British team lacked negotiating capacity and was beset daily by demands from UKIP campaigners, Tory backbenchers and eurosceptic tabloids who did not recognise the complexity of their predicament.

But even considering this, the performance of the Brexit ministers was lamentable: they exhibited a consistent inability to grasp the pace and nature of their task.

The International Trade Secretary Liam Fox started by promising to obtain trade deals with the rest of the world while his colleagues secured an agreement with the EU. In July 2016, he told *The Sunday Times* that 'about a dozen free trade deals outside the EU' would be 'ready for when we leave'.

There was, of course, a problem: Britain could not negotiate or sign a trade deal while a member of the EU. Even if this hadn't been illegal, it would have been illogical. Potential trading partners didn't want to negotiate a trade deal with the UK until they could see what its relationship would be with the single market. Japan, for instance, has 1,000 business in the UK employing around 140,000 people. Those investments are heavily dependent on using Britain as a beachhead for the rest of the single market. Without clear answers on membership, there would be no point in Japan even entering preliminary talks.

Ten days later, Fox quietly retreated on his previous commitments, telling *The Times*: 'We cannot negotiate any new trade deals as long as we are part of the EU which we will probably be for the next two years'. He was admitting that all the statements since he had become the secretary of state had been meaningless.

His position seemed slightly tragic. He had been unceremoniously sacked as defence secretary years beforehand for inviting a friend into confidential Ministry of Defence briefings, after which he had toiled away trying to create support on the backbenches for his hawkish foreign policy proposals. But now that he had clawed his way back into government, it turned out his department was imaginary. He may have been the first British cabinet minister in history to find that it would be illegal for him to carry out his role.

David Davis showed a similar inability to grasp the rudiments of the EU. In May 2016, the last month of the referendum campaign, he wrote on Twitter: 'The first calling point of the UK's negotiator immediately after Brexit will not be Brussels, it will be Berlin, to strike a deal. Post Brexit a UK-German deal would include free access for their cars and industrial goods, in exchange for a deal on everything else. Similar deals would be reached with other key EU nations.' He had still not grasped that it was illegal for EU member states to negotiate or sign bilateral trade deals.

Even after he had been in the job for months, Davis still appeared to be struggling with his brief. He told the House of Commons Foreign Affairs Select Committee that Europe would fare worse than the UK if Article 50 ended without a deal and Britain fell onto WTO rules. This was particularly troubling, because it suggested that he did not understand why Article 50 is so disadvantageous to Britain.

There was a significant improvement when he told the House of Lords Brexit committee: 'This is likely to be the most complicated negotiation of modern times,' suddenly sounding much more wary than before. 'It may be the most complicated negotiation of all time.'

Suddenly, all he could see were troubles – on Scotland and Ireland, on non-tariff agreements and on the law. 'We've got a whole series of economic exercises,' Davis said, 'a whole series of diplomatic exercises, at least 30 interlocutors, the Commission, the Council and the Parliament. We have got the legal analysis to complete and I have to tell you, we have been given 180 degree opposite opinions on some things... Once it really gets underway I suspect the pace of life will be quite hard.'

This suggested the scale of the task was starting to permeate the fog of self-congratulation that had enveloped him and Fox and Johnson. Nevertheless, the time it took for Davis to start talking accurately and realistically was troublingly long. Even when negotiations started in summer 2017 the British team had failed to reach a firm position on a range of key divorce issues such as budget contributions to the EU and the border in Ireland. There was little evidence to suggest that he or his fellow ministers – or indeed the Conservative Party in general – could negotiate the obstacles in their way.

Hopes had been higher for Theresa May. She had survived six years at the Home Office, a department notorious for killing off careers. She had sensibly kept her head down during the referendum, stood back when the ensuing Tory leadership battle turned into a Shakespearian bloodbath and bought herself time by issuing holding statements which pacified both Brexiters and Remainers.

Many people expected her to bring some control and sense to the Brexit process, but despite the overwhelming support of the British eurosceptic press she made error after error. She gave away her leverage over Article 50, had her bid for preliminary talks rejected, and put red lines on issues which she could not deliver.

But all of these errors were as nothing compared to her decision to call a snap general election in summer 2017. By the time it was over, she had alienated European allies, diminished her reputation with the British press, eradicated her own majority in Parliament and fatally undermined her authority. Worst of all, she had squandered months of priceless Article 50 negotiating time. Her misjudgements have gravely undermined Britain's position.

What tools do they have?

The UK is disadvantaged by the Brexit process, but it does have some strengths.

Firstly, it has a robust consumer economy that Europe wants to access. More of the other 27 member states' goods go to the UK (16.9%) than to, say, the US (16.5%). The UK buys £69 billion more in goods and services from the EU than it sells to its countries. Across the EU, 5.8 million jobs are associated with Britain, including 1.3 million in Germany and 500,000 in France.

Brexiters always argued that German carmakers would bang on Chancellor Merkel's door in the wake of a Brexit vote, demanding Britain be given the benefits of the single market at all costs. This was overstated but has some truth. Germany exports about a fifth of all its new cars – 820,000 vehicles last year – to the UK, their single biggest market. Other sectors of German manufacturing will also push for a decent deal.

The reliance of European businesses on the UK has prompted some people to suggest 'they need us more than we need them'. As with all alluring nonsense, it is based on a grain of truth. But the Brexiters have drastically underestimated the complexity and lopsidedness of the relationship. British consumer spending power is important, but it will only go so far in the negotiations.

Our trade with some European Union states is small, but each has the power to block a trade deal. So while we take £60 billion of imports from Germany a year, the figure for Cyprus is £152 million. Cyprus's incentives in the trade deal will be considerably smaller than Germany's, yet politicians in Nicosia will have the same power of veto as those in Berlin.

Take a country like Poland. It exports a healthy £8 billion of goods to the UK annually, but agreeing a tariff-free deal may not make up for the loss of remittance payments from its citizens living in Britain and the humiliation of Poles being barred from moving here. Consumer spending power is important, but it is not a deal-breaker.

The argument also presumes that Europe will think only in economic terms, but this misjudges Britain's partners. European leaders feel they are fighting to secure the survival of their project, a project which they see as a bulwark against war and tyranny. Germany has the most to lose economically by hampering trade with Britain. But even here, only 7.2% of its exports go to Britain. That is a substantial sum, but not necessarily a decisive one when it comes to negotiations on something as crucial as the future of Europe. Angela Merkel threw out business leaders' concerns when she imposed sanctions on Russia. She seems ready to do the same here. The fact that Britain is even pursuing this path demonstrates that politics often trumps economics.

Scale is also an issue. Regardless of how much EU countries export to us, there is still an obvious imbalance in a relationship between a large trading block and one of its members, no matter how wealthy. The EU buys just under half of our total exports, while we take just 8% of its – and about half of that comes from just two states, Germany and the Netherlands. There are several EU states without a trade surplus with the UK.

The idea that Europeans need us more than we need them also assumes that Britons would happily go without – or pay more for – products from the Continent. We rather like our BMWs and Burgundy and may oppose any deal which makes them dearer.

The impact of tariffs also varies by product. In Germany's case, its car industry may not be dented much. After all, these are typically luxury items. Many drivers who can afford an Audi, Mercedes or Porsche won't be put off by a 10% price hike, even if all the extra duty were passed onto the consumer.

Nonetheless, the UK will be able to leverage its spending power, along with the prospect of continued financial stability. Europe does not want trade suddenly blocked, or tailbacks on the border. That would be economically disastrous and politically catastrophic. It would indicate that the European project is unravelling and shake global confidence in Brussels.

But, again, the political impact would be even more devastating for Britain. It would be like two men in a room threatening to shoot themselves, except the EU's gun is pointing at its foot and Britain's gun is pointing at its head. If it comes down to brinkmanship, the EU still holds the stronger hand, even if both partners suffer.

Britain has some strengths away from its credit card wielding shoppers. The UK is western Europe's dominant military power, with considerably more capacity and willingness to engage than its closest competitor, France. Without Britain, the EU is almost defenceless. NATO can take over some of that role, but the American element means it's not a reassuring swap for the Continent.

Continued security cooperation will be a key British offer in the months to come. The Baltic states and Finland are concerned about Russia's territorial ambitions. Military promises might also help appease Poland, which would be badly hurt by UK restrictions on eastern European workers. And as a leading figure in the mid-level groups of EU nations, anything that can get Poland on side will help disproportionately with other member states.

So far the Europeans have presented an impressively united front, but a clever British negotiating team might exploit divisions among them.

Ireland is desperate for the UK to prosper because of its reliance on our economy. The southern European states – France, Italy, Spain, Portugal, Greece, Cyprus and Malta (known as the Club Med countries) – may support British demands in return for support to reform Brussels' fiscal rules. Others may be bought off with security promises. Germany will be tempted by a moderate deal regardless of its car industry, because it and Britain used to work closely in the EU and it's the only country which has been outvoted more often than us. There should be enough residual affection for a reasonable settlement.

Berlin also knows that no-one benefits from a chaotic, hard Brexit. This view is likely to be supported by the fellow pragmatist Donald Tusk at the European Council. But President Macron of France will likely want a tougher deal, as will Jean-Claude Juncker at the European Commission.

All told, this is not a winning deck of cards, but it is not nothing either. Britain remains a strong economic and military power. With canny negotiation, some goodwill, sufficient resources and a sensible timetable, it could secure a decent deal to exit the European Union.

What is the context?

Ministers are operating in an environment that is much more complicated and restrictive than they imagine. They are being forced into an impossible timetable by an overmighty negotiating partner, while trying to establish a society-wide regulatory framework and facing a volatile Parliament with a non-existent majority. And all this is happening against a backdrop of falling economic confidence and growing international concern.

The economy

After the referendum vote, the pound fell to a 31-year low on currency markets. While there have been occasional bounces, the trend has been downwards and there is no sign of sterling reaching its pre-referendum level.

Britons going on holiday abroad have been the first to feel the pain, but that's just the start. The prices of imported goods like food, petrol and electrical goods have risen, without wages going up to compensate. While Brexiters suggested that a weak pound would invigorate exports as British products fell in price abroad, in fact exports have been sluggish.

Fortunately Britain's debts are in its own currency, so the cost of meeting its borrowing does not increase alongside sterling's decline. But the confidence of foreign investors in the British economy is draining away. This is due partly to political instability and the anti-foreigner rhetoric of ministers, but mostly because of fears of a hard Brexit. The higher price of government bonds suggests investors consider the UK to be riskier than they did in May 2016. Reliability and trust are qualities that are hard to gain, but easy to lose. Britain is throwing away its most valuable asset: its reputation.

The City of London

Britain's financial services will weaken as banks move part of their operations and staff to EU jurisdictions in Ireland or mainland Europe. This will not be a rout, but a small and steady leak.

The City of London will survive Brexit. It has many advantages over its European rivals including the English language, and the culture, shopping and diversity of London. It also has no prime competitor on the Continent. No other European financial centre has the capacity to absorb more than a few thousand staff. Frankfurt, for instance, has only one international school.

A bank wanting to move large sections of its operations to another country has to think about how its staff would live. Two hedge funds, Brevan Howard and Blue Crest, moved to Switzerland a few years ago and quickly ran into problems. For a start, many employees refused to go. For those that did, the firms were forced to hire the headmistress of Cheltenham Ladies College to set up a private school for the children of members of staff; there simply weren't enough places in the local school system.

It is also true that Brexit will not damage firms across the board. Most asset management firms in London already operate across the EU, so they will already have some sort of legal entity in Dublin, Luxembourg or elsewhere should Britain fall out of the single market. Most hedge funds, private equity firms and insurance companies will be largely unaffected too, as will retail banking.

However there could be severe problems for UK financial services companies which trade heavily in other European countries. As we saw earlier, the EU's system of passporting allows such firms to sell financial products to customers across the other 27 European Union nations. Losing those passports would block that trade.

Some have suggested that the outcry over the loss of passporting is exaggerated. They argue that a second iteration of the Markets in Financial Instruments Directive, due to come into force in 2018, will save the day. This law allows companies in non-EU countries to trade with the EU if they are granted equivalency status. The idea that this is a good alternative to the current arrangement is wrong: equivalence status can take years to be granted and can be taken away in days.

The fact that the status relies on European cooperation also means that it would only be a reliable fallback option if negotiations with the EU have gone well, which is far from assured. Britain outside the single market will be grateful for the new directive, but it is not equal to passporting. The reality is that losing passporting will batter the British economy.

Investment banking will be hit first and hardest.

European companies operating in London will be fine, although they may need to move a few hundred jobs. For American or Japanese firms treating the UK as a portal to the single market, the effect will be more serious. 87% of US investment bank staff in Europe are in the UK; that number is expected to decline. Those firms will have to set up a subsidiary in Europe, which will require very significant funding to convince regulators it can stand on its own two feet. It is likely that some time after doing so, international bank executives will start asking: 'Do we really need two European offices?' We may not like the answer.

Ultimately big US companies like JP Morgan and Morgan Stanley will be able to afford adapting to a dual UK-EU footing. Things will be much worse for small financial firms. They will face high capital requirements from European regulators that will require substantial sums to be transferred to a new EU office. Many will not be able to afford to do so and will simply stop selling the services, making the market less competitive and depriving them and the Treasury of revenue. Even some larger domestic banks will struggle though, especially if they have concentrated their European activities in London, like Barclays.

There will be no immediate shocks. Financial services will drift towards EU states. Dublin, Paris, Frankfurt, Luxembourg and others will take a few thousand workers each. But after a while economists will look at the cumulative data and find that Brexit cost the City nearly 10% of its capacity, 100,000 jobs and £12 billion in revenue in the first year alone.

Anticipating a bad result, banks have already started moving operations to Europe. That process will continue throughout Article 50. Firms need a long lead time to implement their contingency plans. When HSBC moved its headquarters from London to Birmingham it took three years and that was within the same jurisdiction. Yet the government has kept banks in the dark about its plans. So institutions have begun to act, guided by the principle of no regret decisions. The logic is simple: they cannot afford to risk losing major revenue streams if Britain leaves the single market, so they have moved functions in expectation of it happening.

The most sensible option is to move parts of the business directors wanted to move anyway. That way, if Britain remains in the single market, or somehow manages to secure the ability to operate within it, they have at least made a decision which can be justified on its own terms.

What this means in practice is that low to medium income jobs will be the first to be exported from the UK. Many administrative and back-office jobs will move to cheaper European cities, like Warsaw, where rent is lower and workers are paid less. Many of the UK job losses will not necessarily be in the City at all. Offices in Bournemouth, Glasgow, Belfast and Manchester are at risk.

Some firms will not be able to complete their transfer to Europe before Britain leaves the EU. It is unclear whether European regulators have the capacity to deal with their requests in time and, politically, they may not be welcomed. With memories of the financial crash still fresh, many European central banks are wary of a large UK investment bank striding into their economy. Companies like HSBC come with a two trillion dollar balance sheet, which taxpayers can be saddled with if they collapse.

Immigration

Immigration to the UK fell after the referendum vote and continued to do so thereafter. Although most members of the public don't know it due to decades of tabloid misinformation, this will lower the standard of living. The reason for this is one of the great unsayable elements of British politics: immigration is good for the economy.

The reason it is beneficial is very simple: there are too many old people in Britain.

People's financial relationship with the state works in the following way. They are a net cost at the beginning and end their life and a net contributor in the middle. In childhood they cost money in benefits, schooling and health, and at the end they cost even more in medical bills and pensions. The taxes they pay during their career are essentially a loan repayment for childhood and a downpayment on retirement.

Britain's problem is baby boomers: there are too many of them. We have too many people using up resources at the end of their lives and not enough people of working age paying taxes to make the sums work.

There are several solutions to this, such as training the workforce to a higher standard so that the indigenous population pays more in taxes. But however you tackle the problem, immigration is absolutely key. This has been well documented by the Bank of England, the Office of Budget Responsibility and the Institute of Fiscal Studies.

Immigrants are useful in two respects, economically speaking. Firstly, in general someone else has already paid for their education and training. Those who arrived between 2001 and 2011, for instance, endowed the UK with productive human capital that would have cost it £6.8 billion in education spending. Secondly, they often leave to go back home when they've finished working, meaning even later life costs are sometimes avoided.

Immigrants also tend to make more money, pay more taxes and increase productivity in their sector.

Particular kinds of immigrants are particularly economically beneficial. Foreign students, who are disproportionately likely to be wealthy, well-educated and to start successful businesses, are especially advantageous. They pay large sums of money to attend UK universities. Even when they return home, they are more likely to establish business interests in the UK. But their numbers have declined since the rules on student visas were tightened and are likely to decline even further following the announcement of new measures against them by the government.

Migrants contributed £20 billion to the UK between 2001 and 2011, according to researchers at UCL. The Office for Budget Responsibility puts that contribution in stark terms: by 2062, if annual immigration was 140,000 a year, Britain's public sector net debt-to-GDP ratio will reach 99%; but if the net number of people coming to the UK was zero, it would balloon to 174%. Reducing immigration means the UK will have to cut public services and benefits to make up the shortfall.

The expected fall in immigration during this period will partly be a result of government rhetoric, which has become openly unpleasant. It is also partly to do with the result itself and the perception that the UK is no longer a friendly place for foreigners. And it is partly to do with the spate of racist attacks after the referendum result, which were reported widely overseas. But mostly it is economic.

Migrants go to countries where they think there are job opportunities and where they expect to be treated fairly. As the economy deteriorates, that will be the case less often in Britain. The result of this decline in immigration will be a reduction in welfare and public service funding, triggering either further austerity or tax rises or, more likely, both. Just as prices rise, the public will be paying more tax for fewer services.

This is core to understanding the free movement dynamic: not only will Britain be poorer for leaving the single market to reduce immigration, reducing immigration itself will make Britain poorer too.

Some of those who voted Brexit may expect that at least their wages will rise due to the cut in immigration. Brexiters, including Labour MPs, frequently argue that unskilled immigration depressed low and medium wages. But this is largely false. Many studies find no downward effect on wages. Others find a very small one on lower wages. The Bank of England, for instance, found that there might be a 1.8% drop in income for unskilled or semi-skilled workers – but only in sectors like hospitality where there has been a 10% rise in immigration.

A report from the Resolution Foundation after the referendum found that reducing immigration to the government's aim of around 100,000 would increase the wages of low-paid workers in the sectors most affected by between 0.2% and 0.6% – a figure dwarfed by the 2% expected fall in wage growth if Britain leaves the single market.

This will be the economic context in which ministers operate: consumers growing poorer, the economy shrinking, the deficit looking more dangerous and a migration of financial firms to Europe. It is an ugly, toxic mix. The manner in which this economic pressure translates into political demands is unclear. It would not be surprising to see an effective right-wing politician succeed in heaping blame on immigrants. But it is just possible that it will make ministers more cautious, and could even cause them to think again about leaving the single market.

The Parliamentary battle

For Britain to leave the European Union the government needs to get several massive pieces of legislation through Parliament. But the situation at Westminster is unusually volatile. Both Labour and Tories are internally divided on Brexit – across their MPs, their members and their electoral coalitions.

At the time of writing, a minority Conservative government has found some level of inconsistent support from Labour's leader Jeremy Corbyn for leaving the single market and customs union, but it is not clear how long this support will last. Even if it does, internal protests in the Labour Party, a gradually deteriorating economy, and day to day party political point-scoring means Labour will harry the government during votes in Parliament.

Whoever occupies Downing Street will have a difficult time trying to pass the legislation needed to deliver Brexit unless they have a large working majority. As things stand, there is no support in the Commons for any position, whether it is hard Brexit, soft Brexit or Remain.

Making a new country

While all this is going on, ministers will be forced to try to create the regulatory structure of a newly independent Britain, almost from scratch. It is a massive task that they have barely begun to comprehend, let alone address.

The key problem is that severing Britain's membership of the European Union will also kill off lots of other laws important to everyday life. Britain's membership of the EU is a legal agreement, enshrined in domestic law by the European Communities Act 1972. This states that Britain will follow EU law in areas where Brussels has jurisdiction, such as agriculture. Therefore the European Communities Act 1972 must be repealed for Brexit to take place. Unfortunately, this legislation is also the legal mechanism which gives life to lots of other laws from Brussels. If Britain repealed it, there would suddenly be a black hole in the legal system; nearly half a century of law would vanish. It would be chaos. In vast swathes of policy no-one would know what was legal and what wasn't.

Essentially, British and EU law are like two vines which have been crawling over each other and entwining for 40 years. It looks like one big mess. No-one knows which bits belong to one and which bits to the other.

A solution to this problem has already been announced. As we shall see, it is one of the most dangerous developments in British legal history. It is called the repeal bill.

This piece of legislation will try to fix the problem by taking a legal snapshot and insisting everything stays the same unless the British government repeals something. All existing law –

European or otherwise – stands on the day we leave the EU as it did the day before. Then ministers will, in their own sweet time, remove the bits they don't like. This is the only remotely viable way of solving the legal conundrum, but there are several problems with it: it will not work, it requires much more effort than ministers think, it cannot deliver the thing it is supposed to deliver, it demands the creation of a society-wide regulatory framework the likes of which the government does not have time to create, it threatens to tie up British companies in more red tape than they ever had under the EU, and if it ever comes to pass it will spark the deepest and most widespread lobbying operation ever witnessed in Britain.

The trouble with the repeal bill solution is that not all EU law is in the European Communities Act. This is something right-wing Conservative backbenchers, who often demand we simply repeal the bill and walk away from Europe, have consistently failed to understand. This legislation is not a time machine. Hardline Brexiters often seem to act like they are living in a Doctor Who episode where a quick wiggle of the sonic screwdriver in the right legislative direction will erase the last forty years of legal history. It will not. EU and British law's entanglement is much deeper and more far-reaching than they think.

Somewhere in Whitehall there is probably someone who understands the origin of all the law in each small subject area. With enough time, and enough of the right people in a room, this problem could be fixed. But ministers do not have any time. Since the triggering of Article 50, the clock has been ticking down on filling the unmapped black hole in British law.

Take one bill as an example: the Equalities Act. This was one of the key achievements of the Blair government. It banned discrimination in the provision of goods and services on the basis of age, disability, gender reassignment, marriage and civil partnership, race, religion or belief, sex and sexual orientation. It stitched together several old government bills like the Equal Pay Act 1970 and the Race Relations Act 1976, but it also implemented the four major EU Equal Treatment Directives.

Age discrimination was part of that EU directive. Maybe, if that directive had not existed, New Labour would have banned age discrimination anyway. Maybe it would not have done. But whatever the high politics, the reality is that the provision for age discrimination is from the EU, enacted by the British government in response to an EU directive.

The principle of equal pay for work of equal value is also from the EU. Britain had to improve its existing equal pay law to reach that standard. Race equality was British. It already had that on the statute book. But then the EU adopted a similar law and Britain implemented it. Is that now an EU law or a UK one? It is hard to tell. The origin of a law is not the only pertinent fact. Ministers may also need to establish the chronology.

Some of our laws have been designed specifically to be Brussels friendly. UK competition law, for instance, is modelled on EU competition law, so if we are decoupling our legal systems, should we alter competition law to make it properly domestic?

The legal recognition of EU regulators will prove hugely problematic for ministers. Many of the laws ministers are planning to snapshot bring these regulators into force. They basically state that Britain comes under the jurisdiction of these Continental authorities. Not only must this be changed in law, but new UK regulators will need to be created to replace them, or old ones have powers transferred to them so they can take over their function.

This is one of the most labour-intensive demands of the entire Brexit process. Britain needs to create a regulatory system across swathes of the country's policy agenda. Among many, many others, it must somehow replicate the regulatory functions of agencies like the:

European Court of Auditors
European Data Protection Supervisor
Education, Audiovisual and Culture Executive Agency
Executive Agency for Small and Medium-sized Businesses
Innovation and Networks Executive Agency
European Research Council,
European Agency for Safety and Health at Work
European Aviation Safety Agency
European Centre for Disease Prevention and Control
European Fisheries Control Agency
European Food Safety Authority
European Maritime Safety Agency
European Railway Agency
Office for the Body of European Regulators for Electronic Communication
European Union Statistical Office of the European Communities.

And that's not to mention joint initiatives like Single European Sky.

In some cases that will entail setting up regulators from scratch. In others it will mean bulking up the resources of British regulators which have grown scrawny from under-use. As a project, this will require all the resources of a civil service already stretched to the limit by other aspects of Brexit.

Some hard Brexiters suggest that the way to deal with this problem is to hand it to the courts. A report by the Centre for Social Justice written by Tory MPs John Redwood, Iain Duncan Smith, Owen Paterson, Peter Lilley and William Cash suggested that while Britain builds its own capacity British courts should rule on regulatory standards by following the decisions of European regulators.

It is an absurd solution and one which doesn't survive contact with the real world. Take the European Medicines Agency, which is based in London. Firstly, this agency will undoubtedly move after Brexit, which will have major implications. Many foreign pharmaceutical companies operate in London because the European Medicines Agency is here. They are likely to leave with it.

But that will only be the start of the problems with pharmaceuticals. Drug firms need to submit results to the European Medicines Agency or they can't progress with testing and production for the European market. Post-Brexit they will still be able to go to the agency, wherever it is now located, for drugs intended for Europe. But where will they go to secure authorisation for drugs intended for the UK market now it is outside the remit of the European agency? There is a British medicines authority but will it be ready in time to handle the workload? Have the laws been amended to give it the supervisory powers?

MPs seem to envisage British courts replicating detailed scientific authorisation requirements for the regulation of drugs for sale in the UK market. It is not a task to which judges are particularly well suited. Instead, it is very likely that pharmaceutical firms will simply stop selling their new drugs on the British market until the problem is resolved. A country which is currently one of the global hubs of pharmaceutical development could become an afterthought.

The snapshot solution also only solves the problem of what happens to our domestic law. It offers no guarantee that EU countries will recognise new British law or court rulings on issues like the European arrest warrant, divorces or child maintenance. If a deal is not reached with the EU, European countries could unilaterally decide not to recognise British judgments. Suddenly, a husband who left his wife and child and went to live in Italy wouldn't have to send back his maintenance payments. A woman who divorced her husband and went to live in the Czech Republic would discover her divorce was not legally recognised. The potential for legal mayhem is vast.

This would have a major effect on London's legal industry, much of which is based on foreign claimants wanting a British judgment recognised in another country.

Then once Britain is out the EU, a new set of problems will present themselves, this time to do with excessive red tape – the very thing eurosceptics supposedly abhor.

UK firms selling into the single market will have to keep their standards at the European level regardless of which laws the UK government repeals. In practice it will be cheaper for them to produce all their goods to that standard rather than make one set for Britain and another for Europe.

That situation will be tolerable as long as Britain only ever reduces its standards. Companies that want to sell only nationally can follow British standards, those that want to sell to Europe will follow EU standards. But what happens if the UK increases standards in an area? Say it decides to change the recycling standards on drug packaging, or the requirements on animal welfare in the meat industry. These would both be perfectly commendable things to do, but they would leave domestic exporters in a precarious position.

Now they have to abide by the higher British standard on animal testing, and the higher European standard on everything else. Eventually the divergences will grow, with Britain holding higher standards in some areas and lower standards in others.

Businesses will have twice as much red tape as they had before Brexit. One regulatory system will have been replaced by two. As soon as changes start being made, big business will be feverishly campaigning for the government to stick to the EU standard.

But not all businesses have the same incentives. Small-and-medium-sized businesses are likely to campaign for relief from existing regulations because they sell mostly to a domestic market.

While talks are ongoing, the law will stay as it is. But industry lobby groups will be aware that once the repeal bill comes into force they will have a once-in-a-lifetime opportunity to secure changes to government policy they've always dreamed of, or the battle-of-a-lifetime to prevent changes to government policy they've always dreaded. The Article 50 period will be characterised by ferocious lobbying across policy areas.

The incentives here are not clear cut. Reforming one bit of regulation can lead to changes in an entirely unrelated part of the economy. Take the Working Time Directive, which guarantees that workers cannot be forced to work more than 48 hours a week by their employer. It is an historic object of complaint of British eurosceptics, despite promises not to water down workers' rights.

Should ministers water it down, the repercussions will soon hit the NHS. Britain originally excluded parts of the health service from the Working Time Directive, largely because it could only function by over-working junior doctors. But two court cases in the early 2000s amended that exemption. Under the current law, the time doctors spend on call in their workplace is classified as working time.

Any reform to that system will trigger protests and possibly even strikes from junior doctors. The British Medical Association will throw its considerable weight behind them. And that lobbying operation will be mimicked in nearly every industry and sector in the British economy. This will be a feeding frenzy for those trying to influence government policy.

To get a sense of the complexity of the problems that will confront ministers, let's look at just one area of British life: animals. Exploring three different aspects of our experience of animals – veterinary services, farming and fishing – will give a sense of the task ahead. Doing so also allows us to see how the various working parts of Brexit affect one another. In this book we have mostly looked at the elements of Britain's withdrawal from Europe in separation. But part of the complexity is that ministers will be trying to formulate policy in one area while Brexit plays havoc with interrelated ones. Everything affects everything else.

Veterinary medicine

Let's take veterinary services first. The Royal College of Veterinary Surgeons and the British Veterinary Association have warned that a sudden reduction in immigration would damage animal services in the UK. Half of veterinary surgeons registering to practise in the UK are from overseas, with the vast majority coming from the EU.

This reduction would be felt unevenly. Plenty of people would still train to become family vets; everyone loves the idea of treating a cute dog and seeing the look of joy in a family's eyes when it recovers. The problem lies in the less romantic parts of veterinary services: TB testing, meat hygiene and veterinary surveillance in abattoirs.

Industry estimates suggest that 95% of vets in meat hygiene graduated elsewhere in the EU. British vets simply do not like the work. The problem is not only that it is more poorly paid, though it is. The trouble is that someone willing to go through the extensive training requirements of veterinary medicine generally does not do so in order to spend their working life watching animals being killed.

Critics who say Britain should be training up more indigenous workers to do these roles have two difficulties. Firstly, there is a time-lag. Training vets takes years and the country won't be sure that it requires this domestic intake until the conclusion of Article 50. By the time we know we need them, it will be too late. Secondly, it is not clear whether there are enough British people who want to go through all that training and take on all that student debt to oversee the slaughter of animals.

However, if those roles are not filled, the UK has real problems. Firstly, it will not be able to export meat products to the EU, because an independent veterinary presence in the abattoir is one of the standards imposed by Brussels.

Secondly, it is a public health threat. Infectious diseases like foot and mouth, avian influenza and BSE are often spotted in abattoirs, either when the animal first arrives or in meat inspections. A shortage of veterinary services in abattoirs increases the likelihood of another outbreak.

If an outbreak does occur, the UK will be handling it without funding from the EU, which provides for rapid action and contributes towards compensation. It may also be going without the advice provided by the EU, especially if it chooses to step outside of disease surveillance and eradication projects in which it works hand-in-hand with European partners.

Finally, there is an ethical problem. As consumers become more aware of animal rights issues, they demand greater assurances about the welfare of the animals slaughtered for their food. A veterinary presence in the meat industry provides an independent set of eyes and ears concerned with animal welfare, not profit. It's the type of thing people want more of, not less.

Veterinary services could also be damaged if the UK steps out of the Veterinary Medicinal Products Directive. If the UK adopts a different model and ends its parity with the EU system, it will suddenly have a completely different system for manufacturing, marketing and monitoring veterinary medicines. As a comparatively small market, that means companies may not bother selling new products in the UK.

It is for this reason that, despite all the noise, ministers are likely to once again try and keep things exactly as they were before. Just as we saw at the WTO, the substantive rules which govern trade and industry are likely to be left as untouched as humanly possible, in order to keep things stable. But the immigration problem will need to be addressed, or else it could be extremely damaging to trade, public health and animal welfare.

Farming

Britain will regain control of lawmaking in agriculture. For years rural communities and eurosceptic MPs have complained that the EU interferes too much in farming, forcing farmers to obey regulations on tail-docking pigs or livestock movements.

It is possible that the deal with the EU would uphold many of these rules. But even if not, 38% of the UK's total production of sheep and lamb goes to the EU. Anyone selling into the European market will have to make products to its standards.

Leaving the EU will have a significant impact on tariffs, which can be sky high on animal products. As David Cameron said during the campaign, farmers could face tariffs of 13% on salmon, 40% on lamb and 70% on beef.

There will also be problems for parts of the agricultural industry – especially horticulture – if there is a significant clamp down on immigration. Many sectors, such a fruit-picking, rely on migrant workers.

Devolution will deepen the problems. After Brexit, Scotland, Wales and Northern Ireland will be free to pursue their own independent policies in farming. Perhaps one will try to undercut the rest of the UK on standards and costs. Perhaps another will offer more protection to agriculture. It's hard to tell. But whichever way it goes, it will transform UK agriculture.

This will all take place under the supervision of a weakened and diminished government department. Agriculture has been under European control for so long that the Department for the Environment, Food and Rural Affairs (Defra) is one of Whitehall's smallest ministries. Its modest team of civil servants will struggle to cope. That could prove a serious problem for farmers when it comes to the thorny issue of subsidies, which have been guaranteed by ministers for the next few years. What happens after that is unclear.

With a weak government department and gradually declining public finances, the prospects for retaining the subsidies do not look good. If they end, some types of farming will decline. Farms concerned with livestock like beef and sheep would be particularly vulnerable. More intensive sectors like poultry and pigs, which receive less subsidy, would probably survive. Cereals are likely to struggle. The suffering of the industry will be more severe if, as free market eurosceptics want, Britain's borders are simultaneously opened to cheap exports from third countries.

Fishing

When Britain leaves the EU we will regain control over own waters, like any other independent country. In practical terms that means we control economic activity taking place up to 200 miles out to sea. Technically, Britain could tear up all the EU agreements it has with other states and bar other countries from fishing in those waters.

The trouble is that if Britain does this other countries would bar it from fishing in their waters. This would not suit the British palate. Although cod in fish and chips can come from the North Sea, most of our white fish comes from the seas around Iceland and Norway. Meanwhile, Britain exports most of the shellfish caught in its own waters such as langoustine, scallops and crab.

To prevent overfishing, Europe's fisheries policy makes countries share stocks with varying degrees of geographical access. Fish swim all over territorial boundaries but each member state is given a quota of the stock it is entitled to catch.

The quotas were set years ago and have caused an awful lot of upset ever since. Politics, as always with the EU, crept into what should really have been a discussion about numbers and demand. Britain in particular was thought to have got a bad deal. This partly explains why the fishing industry was so stridently pro-Brexit during the campaign.

The quotas are converted into yearly limits of how much of a species each country can catch and where it can do so. Each year, scientists estimate a sustainable catch and the Council of Ministers thrashes out the total allowable catch for each country. Before the Council meets, the EU shares out the North Sea stocks with Norway. Britain may try to insert itself into that meeting once it has left the EU. Meanwhile, the west of Scotland, the Irish Sea and the Channel would ideally become bilateral matters between the UK and the EU. This part may be relatively straightforward, although it would be easy for the EU to make it difficult if there is no goodwill.

Britain may also try to negotiate bigger fish quotas for UK fishermen.

Economically, fishing is less important now than it was when the quotas were first set, but emotionally and politically it is much stronger. Its resonance in the Brexit campaign as an industry let down by Brussels means it has the ear of ministers.

These talks will use up a lot of time and energy from Europe. They are not simple discussions. As one Norwegian marine scientist once remarked: 'Managing cod stocks is not rocket science. It is much more complicated than that.'

Britain will be trying to re-establish its share of the continent's fish. It is no small task. And it will have very few civil servants qualified to make its case. As ever, politics from other areas of the EU will influence the discussions. Nations usually get very bullish about their access. Environmentalists fear that any breakdown in talks may trigger a spasm of over-fishing as regulation disintegrates.

Civil servants would love to do here what they will do elsewhere and simply mimic the existing quotas to make the Brexit transition as stable as possible. But they won't be able to. The role of fishermen in the Brexit campaign was too prominent. Ministers may well be forced to prise open a highly-technical rationing system for a constantly-moving resource, even though they have neither the negotiating capacity nor the desire to do so. And they will be expected to come back with a good deal at the end of it.

So even in this relatively small area of the animal world it is clear that ministers have an extraordinarily complicated task to complete. They must address a capacity problem in veterinary services, secure the ability of the meat industry to export to Europe, safeguard meat inspection processes, handle the lobbying from the farming industry to change EU rules, address fears over sudden tariff rises in key meat export sectors, manage the potentially explosive effects of devolution, make existential decisions on the maintaining of farm subsidies, and then open and successfully negotiate complex international discussions on fish stocks. And all during a period of economic uncertainty when all civil service capacity is directed towards the process of leaving the EU.

The Brexit negotiations may be the most important Britain has held since the war. But they will take place against a backdrop of tumultuous and deep-rooted change across society and industry.

The time problem

The cruellest element is time. There is just not enough of it. Two years might just have been enough to complete the administrative element of Article 50. It is not enough to recreate the EU's regulatory infrastructure or to negotiate, agree and ratify a good trade deal. Anyone trying to complete these tasks competently would probably need ten years.

One way to buy more time would be to try to extend Article 50, but the government has refused to entertain this. Ministers have portrayed suggestions they do so as a cynical attempt to sidestep the will of the people. It is unclear whether this is an excuse or paranoia, but either way, the failure to secure a time extension puts Britain at risk of a chaotic Brexit and gives Europe the advantage of knowing our back is up against the wall during the negotiations.

Another sensible solution to the time problem would be to sign up to an interim EEA option, keeping Britain in the single market and customs union. This would immediately remove the cliff edge of a hard Brexit, create a more sensible period to negotiate a trade deal and keep the economy chugging along pretty much as before. Businesses who currently feel the need to move because of the uncertainty would stay put.

There are downsides. Staying in the EEA, even as an interim agreement, would involve accepting freedom of movement and contributing to the EU budget. The hard rump of the Brexit brigade – the right-wing tabloids, UKIP campaigners and Tory backbenchers – would say the government is trying to avoid implementing the referendum result. Downing Street would have to face them down bravely – a quality it does not currently seem to have. But that is a short-term political calculation. The negative headlines of an interim deal would be nothing compared to the daily headlines of mass job losses if Britain fell out the single market without a trade deal.

An interim EEA option also demands a lot from Britain's negotiating partners. Falling into EEA membership is not as simple as just saying so. It would still take considerable negotiation. And Britain would be demanding that, after investing resources to secure that deal, EU leaders would then have to start a second round of talks to strike a final settlement. In truth, the period in which this might have been achieveable has probably passed.

If so, it was a significant missed opportunity. The interim EEA option was recommended by pretty much everyone who understood the stakes of a hard Brexit, from dyed-in-the-wool Leavers concerned about the cliff edge, to the Remainers desperately looking to minimise the damage of the vote. It was backed by *The Financial Times*, Chatham House, the Adam Smith Institute and countless others. Nevertheless, it never won support from Brexit hardliners, who saw it as a trap by Remainers.

There is one other way of extending the time available to British negotiators and this is the one the government is currently pursuing. It is to request that all existing agreements on tariffs, regulators and rules be 'grandfathered' until replacements have been found. In other words, you would leave the EU in name only, while negotiations continued. From a ministerial perspective this has the advantage of reassuring Brexit supporters that the UK had left the EU, while maintaining financial stability and relieving the time pressure.

In a speech in Florence in September 2017, Theresa May asked for a transition of around two years on existing terms of membership. In truth, even this plan was laughably optimistic. The negotiations for a comprehensive trade agreement between the UK and the EU are likely to last much longer than two years.

Many commentators here and on the Continent were baffled by the government's continued resistance to pursuing an extension of the timetable. The seeming idiocy of this led some to develop conspiracy theories. Jacek Rostowsky, Poland's former minister of finance and deputy prime minister, posited that the Brexit team was hoping to storm off from negotiations so that its weak negotiating position would not be revealed to voters who had been misled during the referendum.

Such imaginative explanations are rarely correct. Most of the time in politics, the simplest explanation is the best one. And the simplest explanation is that the Brexit ministers came to believe their own nonsense. They spent so long beating their chests about British trading prowess and so long insisting that leaving Europe would be simple, so long mocking Remainers for warning of the difficulty of Brexit, that they started ignoring any suggestion to the contrary. This would explain the advice to industry figures about to meet David Davis to be ebullient about Brexit.

In a sense, Brexiters are the EU's ideal negotiators. They are so focused on their own superiority that they do not recognise that it increases their vulnerability. However they find themselves under unprecedented domestic and international pressure. At home, opposition parties are increasingly animated by public anxiety about economic decline. Internationally, global partners like Japan are exhorting the UK to commit to staying in the single market. The pressure will grow and grow.

The eventual outcome of talks is extremely difficult to predict. At the time of writing, the plan is for a two year transition up to 2021, to allow Britain time to negotiate a comprehensive trade agreement. In truth, these transitional arrangements may last so long that the forces driving Brexit weaken. Perhaps the reduction in immigration will make taking back control of our borders less important. Perhaps the continued economic decline caused by the referendum will force the government to keep Britain in the single market, or even make it rethink Brexit altogether.

Alternatively, a sudden and unforeseen event, like the return of Greece's fiscal calamity, may push the UK further from the Continent.

What is definitely the case is that Britain's government has approached Brexit ineptly, misjudging its opponent, underestimating the challenges, and prioritising its short-term political interests over the long-term interests of the country. Ministers threw away their leverage and failed to neutralise the advantages held by the EU. Through a mixture of ignorance and ideological frenzy they have pushed Britain towards a hard, chaotic Brexit.

What happens after Brexit?

The threat from Brexit is not just about economic calamity. It is also a threat to Parliamentary sovereignty, the very principle Brexiters claimed to be fighting for during the referendum.

In the repeal bill, there are legal devices called statutory instruments. Deploying one allows ministers to change the law without having to pass a whole new act through Parliament. Statutory instruments are supposed to be used for uncontroversial updates to legislation – little administrative tasks, like legally recognising a new type of speed camera.

But increasingly they are being used to push through controversial changes. Towards the end of 2014, the government used one to ban certain kinds of pornography from video on demand and tried to make changes to the electoral registration system that angered transgender people.

According to Downing Street, statutory instruments in the repeal bill give the government 'the flexibility to take account of the negotiations with the EU as they proceed'.

In one sense, this is reasonable. Exiting the European Union is so complicated it would be impossible to achieve without statutory instruments. But it is also incredibly dangerous. Ministers suddenly have the power to tinker with nearly half a century of law and industrial standards. Everything is there, from British environmental policy to employment rights to consumer protections.

There will be no European law to stop ministers and no bill to be justified on the floor of the House of Commons or in a TV studio. On a rainy Friday afternoon ministers will be able to make bits of law vanish. The Government has promised it will not do this, but its bill contained very few restrictions and some extraordinarily broad powers.

There is a further cause for concern. Once out of the EU, Britain will seek trade deals with large countries with whom we will be the junior partner. Economically, we may need to turn things around urgently after the sudden shock imposition of tariff and non-tariff barriers. Politically, the government will be desperate to prove that it can, in Theresa May's words, 'make a success' of this venture. So the UK will be put in a vulnerable position precisely when other nations start opportunistically demanding lower industrial standards.

Pharmaceuticals will go first. That is the rule. In US trade negotiations, the pharmaceuticals industry is one of the most influential around. American pharma giants have an incredibly powerful and well-established lobbying operation. Trade deals have been in danger of collapse in Congress because they did not like them. Their acceptance is a precondition of a successful US trade negotiation.

The industry has long looked at the NHS with undisguised appetite. Contrary to left-wing conspiracy theories, the pharmaceutical industry does not hate the NHS. It does not care where the money comes from. What it hates is NICE, the National

Institute for Health and Care Excellence. NICE compares quality and price, which is a disaster for the drug industry.

US pharmaceutical firms are likely to demand the abolition, or at least the reform, of NICE. As a consequence, drug prices will rise. The full effects will only be felt years later. But a decade on, say, the health service's already precarious finances will come under intolerable strain from the extra costs.

This will not be blamed on Brexit. By then there will presumably be another government and another opposition and it will not be in their interests to pin the blame on events from 15 or 20 years ago. The opposition will blame the government of the day, because that is what oppositions do – and the government will blame anyone but the government of the day, because that is what governments do. But the causes of that crisis will be Brexit.

Silicon Valley also exerts huge influence in US trade deals. American tech firms are increasingly outraged by the EU's data protection rules, not least the controversial right to be forgotten, which Google launched a failed action against in early 2016. Firms are also being asked by the EU to specify how they use people's data, automatically allow people to migrate their data to new providers, inform customers and governments of data breaches and demonstrate how they are protecting private data. If they fail, they can be fined 4% of their global revenue. Silicon Valley will be seeking ways to avoid this. US negotiators will demand that the UK reduces its data protection standards from an EU to a US level.

The same pressure will be applied across all industries. Take REACH, the European regulation on the Registration, Evaluation, Authorisation & Restriction of Chemicals. Its guiding principle is that where there is a lack of evidence about the safety of a chemical, it cannot be used until it can be shown to be safe. The American system has the opposite approach: where there is no evidence to demonstrate harm, the chemical is allowed until proven otherwise. US negotiators will push for the UK to adopt the American standard.

In some cases, standards may be protected by our deal with Europe. EU leaders are not going to accept untested chemicals into their market. So Britain will either have to reject the US request and risk the deal, or carve out sectors of its economy where it is producing, importing and exporting to different standards.

In other treaties, the talks will not be so much about reducing standards as accepting the required policy of the negotiating government. In negotiations with India, for instance, immigration is likely to feature. Indian students often find it hard to come to the UK and that has not become any easier since a crackdown on student visas. Despite all the talk of cutting immigration, UK negotiators will come under strain to make concessions in return for a trade deal.

With China, the concern will be energy security. Beijing is likely to demand a greater role in the provision of our energy infrastructure. The government's decision to authorise the Hinkley Point C nuclear power plant, where the Chinese committed to one-third of the £18 billion cost, gave them a foothold in western Europe, as well as a stake in a new project at Sizewell and the possibility of building their own reactors at Bradwell, Essex. China will petition for more access to the market.

This is the reality of trade talks. Sovereignty will be bartered for commerce. Brexiters will tell you that this is different to the

EU because voters can always kick out the government that conducted the negotiations and repeal any deal it made. In reality this very rarely happens. Once a trade deal is signed, it is almost never reversed. That sovereignty stays sold.

Britain is about to experience a toxic mix of weak law and strong lobbying. It is tantamount to switching a country off and on again. Except that it will not revert to its original state. Outside of the single market, and without the protections of EU rules, it will be pushed towards a low-tax, low-regulation laissez faire economy, more akin to that of Singapore or Hong Kong than the countries on the Continent.

The idea that Britain has grown stronger by leaving the EU will be seen as a bad joke when it is being bounced from pillar to post by bigger negotiating partners. Any notion that control has been taken back will seem absurd. Sovereignty will pass from Brussels, over the heads of the British people, into the negotiating rooms of Washington, Beijing and New Delhi.

Postscript

There is an urgent need for some patience and good sense in Britain's current political debate.

Sovereignty is a fine and decent value to pursue in international relations. It is not, as some supporters of the EU have occasionally portrayed it, a foolish and unloved academic concept. People do care about politics, even if they do not always talk about it in the terms used at Westminster. And they feel that they should be in control of their lives, local community, and national laws.

But absolute sovereignty is a fantasy. The only absolute sovereignty available in the world is North Korea's model of total isolation. Outside of that, we must make compromises in order to cooperate with other countries for our mutual advantage. Sometimes these take the form of shared global standards, intelligence sharing or a court governing a single market. One can come to different conclusions as to how far these things should go, but for each step we should be thinking about the competing goods of independence and cooperation.

Sometimes we may feel the loss of independence has gone too far. At other times we may feel we will live better, safer, richer lives by working more closely with others, which will always involve giving up some control. The key thing is to approach the problem by accepting that politics is made of competing goods. It is made of compromises.

Very few of the dangers identified in this book are innately to do with Brexit. They are predominantly about the manner in which Brexit is being pursued. Even if there were widespread public support for us to be out the EU, the single market and the customs union, which is far from proven, it would be relatively straightforward to organise a realistic transitional period in which a decent and comprehensive trade deal could be agreed in the national interest.

Instead, we have been driven towards the cliff edge. This is partly because of political self-interest and partly due to a new and unsettling form of nationalist hysteria among the political class. Once this attitude has been adopted, obstacles start to look like conspiracies and those who point to them start to resemble traitors.

The current debate about Britain's departure from the European Union is being conducted entirely in black and white terms, as if each man were an island, and as if an island is all that Britain is. There is an urgent need for nuance and sober reflection.

Ultimately, it is British values which will help get the country through this difficult new period: calm debate, instinctive scepticism, practical judgement and moderation. We appear to have lost sight of these values. The sooner we reaffirm our commitment to them, the better off we will be.

The Experts

This book is based on conversations with...

James Chalmers
Regius professor of Law at the University of Glasgow

Larry Elliott
Economics editor at *The Guardian*

Sir Lawrence Freedman
Emeritus professor of War Studies at King's College London
and expert in strategic studies

Carl Gardner
Barrister and former government lawyer

Holger Hestermeyer
Shell reader in International Dispute Resolution at the Dickson
Poon School of Law

Markus W. Gehring
Lecturer at the Law Faculty in Cambridge University, fellow
and director of Studies in Law at Hughes Hall, and deputy
director of the Centre for European Legal Studies.

Dominic Grieve
MP for Beaconsfield and former attorney general for England
and Wales and advocate general for Northern Ireland

Sir Paul Jenkins
Barrister at Matrix Chambers, former head of the Government
Legal Department and permanent secretary to the attorney
general

Sabine Jenni
Associated researcher at European Politics Research Group at ETH Zurich and lecturer at the University of Lucerne

Steve Keen
Head of the School of Economics, History and Politics at Kingston University

Guy Lougher
Head of the EU and Competition Law Group at Pinsent Masons.

David Martin
Labour MEP for Scotland and the European Parliament's second-longest serving MEP

Anand Menon
Professor of European Politics and Foreign Affairs at King's College London and director of UK in a Changing EU.

Giles Merritt
Founder and director of Friends of Europe and former Brussels correspondent for *The Financial Times*

Laurent Pech
Professor of European Law, Jean Monnet chair of European Public Law and head of the Law and Politics Department at Middlesex University London

Steve Peers
Professor of EU, Human Rights and World Trade Law at the University of Essex

Gavin Phillipson
Professor of Law at the University of Durham

Keith Rockwell
Director of Information and Media Relations Division at the World Trade Organisation

Roland Smith
Fellow at the Adam Smith Institute

Robert Tombs
Professor of history at Cambridge University and author of *The English and Their History*

David Torrance
Columnist for *The Herald* and author of *Nicola Sturgeon: A Political Life*

Sean Tuffy
Senior vice president and head of Regulatory Intelligence at Brown Brothers Harriman

Alan Winters
Professor of Economics at the University of Sussex and director of the UK Trade Policy Observatory

William Wright
Founder of New Financial and former editor of Financial News

...and others in Westminster, Brussels and Whitehall who asked not to be named.

Acknowledgements

There are many people to thank for this book, but the most important are my friends, family and work colleagues, and in particular my poor parents, who had to listen to me bang on about the World Trade Organisation, poultry exports and the hideousness of politicians on evenings that might otherwise have been pleasant. For this I apologise.

I thank Martin Hickman, my publisher, and Lisa Moylett, my agent. Martin came to me after my first post-referendum blog on Brexit, *Everything You Need To Know About Theresa May's Brexit Nightmare In Five Minutes*, despite the fact that it didn't tell the reader everything they needed and couldn't be read in five minutes. He was generous enough to look past these shortcomings and commission a book. Lisa is a marvel of wit, generosity and good humour who always has your back.

Three people really went above and beyond in helping me make this book as accurate as possible, despite it being written to a tight deadline against a backdrop of evolving events: Holger Hestermeyer, Anand Menon and Steve Peers. They gave up their time to look over sections and point out where I was going wrong, what was going to be embarrassing if anyone other than themselves saw it, and what I had failed to notice. Holger and Anand in particular have been around from the days immediately after the vote, showing extraordinary patience while I tried to understand trade law and always taking time to walk me through an issue without ever seeming as bored and exasperated as they must have been. I have promised you many drinks in exchange for knowledge, gentlemen, and I will deliver.

Finally, thank you to friend and foe on Twitter. You keep me on my toes.

Although I have done my best to keep mistakes to an absolute minimum, such a wide-ranging and current book is bound to contain some. If you spot something which you think is wrong or questionable, email me at iandunt23@gmail.com. I will publish any substantial objections to my facts or reasoning at www.iandunt.com and analyse if they are valid.

References

Introduction

The EU has mutual recognition agreements with Australia, Canada, China, Israel, Japan, New Zealand and the United States, mimicking the bureaucracy-free trade on the Continent.
More details about mutual recognition agreements are available on the European Commission's website (http://ec.europa.eu/growth/single-market/goods/international-aspects/mutual-recognition-agreements_en) (http://europa.eu/rapid/press-release_IP-14-555_en.htm)

By 2030 GDP has reduced by 4.5%.
This is the average of three studies by the Treasury, the think tank NIESR and the Centre for Economic Performance and London School of Economics. (https://www.theguardian.com/politics/2016/oct/18/theresa-may-given-stark-warning-about-leaving-customs-union)

Cars heading from Britain to Europe – almost half the vehicles made in the UK – are hit by a 10% tariff.
The car industry accounts for 10% of the UK's trade in goods and maintains 700,000 British jobs. (www.smmt.co.uk/wp-content/uploads/sites/2/ SMMT-KPMG-EU-Report.pdf) If you want to read the full list of current EU tariffs, which isn't necessarily recommended, you can do so here: (http://eur-lex.europa.eu/legal-content/EN/TXT/?uri=OJ%3AL%3A2015%3A285%3ATOC)

Within a year, the City has lost 100,000 jobs and £12 billion in revenue.
These figures are at the top end of estimates in a PWC report for TheCityUK. (https://www.thecityuk.com/assets/2016/Reports-PDF/Leaving-the-EU-Implications-for-the-UK-FS-sector.pdf)

What did we vote for?

The £350 million figure was misleading.
For a full account of the reality of British funding of the EU, read the IFS report on the subject, published during the referendum campaign (https://www.ifs.org.uk/uploads/publications/bns/BN181.pdf#)

For many Leave voters, money was less important than sovereignty.
Lord Ashcroft's polling revealed a nation deeply divided by age, education, life chances and values (www.lordashcroftpolls.com/2016/06/how-the-united-kingdom-voted-and-why/)

After the referendum, Nigel Farage, leader of the UK Independence Party, said voters had given a mandate to a points-based system for immigration.
Nigel Farage said on 5 September 2016: 'The people were clear in wanting a points based immigration system which is why so many went out and voted to leave the European Union. Any watering down from that will lead to real anger.' (http://www.express.co.uk/news/politics/707277/points-based-immigration-system-uk-australian-style-what-is-theresa-may)

Britain's newly installed Secretary of State for Exiting the European Union, David Davis, was claiming mandates for all sorts of things while unceremoniously dumping the £350 million NHS pledge.
'I made no such pledge,' David Davis told the House of Commons Foreign Affairs Committee on 13 September 2016 when asked about the 'Let's fund the NHS instead' slogan. 'Some did and if you want them to argue the case you should invite the people here who made that argument. You will find in no speech of mine any reference to that.'

Once you drill down into the Brexit mandate, something interesting happens.
For an in-depth analysis of the 'liberal Brexit' vote see Roland Smith's blog on the subject: 'Sizing the Liberal Leave position' (https://medium.com/@WhiteWednesday/sizing-the-liberal-leave-position-858b0259547)

'Facts don't work. You have got to connect with people emotionally. It's the Trump success.'
Arron Banks was quoted in an interview with *The Guardian* on 29 June 2016. (www.theguardian.com/politics/2016/jun/29/leave-donor-plans-new-party-to-replace-ukip-without-farage)

What is Article 50?

'I wrote Article 50, so I know it well.'
Giuliano Amato was quoted by Reuters on 21 July 2016 (http://www.reuters.com/article/us-britain-eu-amato-idUSKCN1012Q8)

Liam Fox went so far as to call the EU migrants in the UK 'one of our main cards'.
Fox made the comments on EU nationals during the Conservative party conference in October 2016. (http://news.sky.com/story/eu-nationals-in-uk-one-of-our-main-cards-in-brexit-deal-liam-fox-10605533)

As the Home Office's own calculations have shown, 80% of EU migrants will be entitled to permanent residency by 2019.
The position of EU migrants was reported by *The Daily Telegraph* and later confirmed in the Commons by David Davis (www.telegraph.co.uk/news/2016/10/07/every-eu-migrant-can-stay-after-brexit-600000-will-be-given-amne/)

'You're not laughing now, are you?'
Nigel Farrage's victory speech to the European Parliament on 28 June 2016, the week after the referendum, was widely reported including by the BBC (http://www.bbc.co.uk/news/uk-politics-eu-referendum-36651406#)

As soon as he was appointed, Fox was forecasting that the European Union would 'sacrifice at least one generation of young Europeans on the altar of the single currency'.
Fox's warning that the European Union would implode was quoted by *The Daily Telegraph* on 28 September 2016 (http://www.telegraph.co.uk/news/2016/09/28/european-union-will-implode-when-britain-leaves-says-liam-fox/)

What is the European project?

After the referendum, Britain had about 40 people who could do the job.
These estimates were made by Lord Price, the minister for trade and investment. Some believed at the time that Britain had no active trade negotiators at all outside of Brussels. (www.telegraph.co.uk/business/2016/07/03/government-faces-worldwide-hunt-for-trade-negotiators-experts-wa/)

Almost as soon as this structure was set up, divisions emerged.
Boris Johnson and Liam Fox clashed after the trade secretary tried to poach some of his colleague's remit, forcing the prime minister to break away from her holiday to scold them both. (http://blogs.spectator.co.uk/2016/08/theresa-may-wont-surprised-liam-fox-boris-johnson-already-battling/)

What is the single market?

After all, what was the point of ensuring qualifications for services like dentistry or hairdressing were recognised all over the Continent if people couldn't travel to sell them?

While freedom of goods, people and capital are very well established, the reality of the single market in services is that progress is slow. Ironically it is Britain which has done most to press the case in this area, and it is now likely to shudder to a halt.

Take Cassis de Dijon.

The full story behind the case can be read here (http://www1.american.edu/TED/cremecassis.htm)

By the time Johnson was finished, Brussels reports had turned into a journalistic genre.

Boris Johnson's Brussels reports didn't just influence the UK. Some believe that they led Danish voters to reject the Maastricht Treaty (http://uk.reuters.com/ article/uk-britain-eu-boris-idUKKCN0W33ZS)

What are the politics of the European Union?

Think for instance of the 56% Leave vote in Cornwall.

Cornwall's Leave vote is seen as a symbol of the self-harm many communities perpetrated on themselves when they voted Leave. (www.theguardian.com/uk-news/2016/jun/26/cornwall-fears-loss-of-funding-after-backing-brexit)

The Commission and the Council even had a territorial dispute over who would take the lead in Brexit negotiations.

The Brussels power struggle over who would lead the negotiations with Britain is detailed here (http://www.politico.eu/article/brussels-power-struggle-over-brexit-negotiations/)

The approval of a recent Canada-EU trade deal – negotiated over several years – was put in jeopardy when member states were involved in its ratification.

Jean-Claude Junker threatened to force through the adoption process without national parliament participation, but Sigmar Gabriel, Germany's economy ministers, branded the idea 'incredibly foolish'. (www.ft.com/content/8e9428d4-412a-11e6-9b66-0712b3873ae1)

When it does want to get a story out about itself it goes to the press corps.
For a breakdown of the Brussels press corps see (http://cleareurope.
eu/10-things-need-know-brussels-press-corps/)

He is an advocate of offering countries associate status.
Guy Verhofstadt has regularly cited this idea as a solution to the EU's
problems, not least in this Politico article before the referendum and a
conversation with Channel 4 news anchor Jon Snow after it (http://www.
politico.eu/article/an-eu-for-full-members-only/) (https://www.youtube.
com/watch?v=PQGf8kDHvi8)

*They're said by European Parliament insiders to talk on the phone several times
a day.*
Jean-Claude Juncker does not always seem particularly happy about these
early morning phone calls, as he made clear in this interview. (http://www.
spiegel.de/international/europe/interview-with-jean-claude-juncker-and-
martinschulz-a-1102110.html)

*She gave it away, seemingly as an afterthought, during a Sunday morning polit-
ical interview in October 2016.*
Theresa May mentioned the deadline she set herself on BBC TV's Andrew
Marr programme, before informing her party conference about it later that
day. (http://www.bbc.co.uk/news/uk-politics-37532364)

*Even during the referendum campaign, David Davis was telling audiences that
EU member states could sign their own trade deals.*
The Secretary of State for Exiting the European Union has at least had the
good grace not to delete the tweets in which he made these errors. (https://
twitter.com/daviddavismp/ status/735770127564607489)

What will we do about freedom of movement?

Bruegal released a report arguing that the EU should concede on this point.
The Bruegal paper caused outrage in Europe for going against the consensus
on protecting free movement at all costs, but some several senior figures
who were more sympathetic in private (http://bruegel.org/2016/08/
europe-after-brexit-a-proposal-for-a-continental-partnership/)

An emergency brake on immigration was 'certainly one of the ideas now on the table'.

The Observer reports cited 'senior British and EU sources' (https://www.theguardian.com/world/2016/jul/24/ brexit-deal-free-movement-exemption-seven-years)

Recent court cases in Germany have seen Romanians who failed to look for work before claiming benefits sent back to their home country.

The case of Dano v Jobcenter Leipzig on 11 November 2014 confirmed that member states had no responsibility to pay social benefits to anyone who had been in another member state without trying to find work for over three months. Anyone staying longer than that needed to demonstrate that they could support themselves and their family members. (https:// www.freemovement.org.uk/dano-and-the-exclusion-of-inactive-eu-citi- zens-from-certain-non-contributory-social-benefits/)

But it does have some high level support.

Nicolas Sarkozy said: 'I would tell the British, you've gone out, but we have a new treaty on the table so you have an opportunity to vote again. But this time not on the old Europe, on the new Europe. Do you want to stay? If yes, so much the better. Because I can't accept to lose Europe's second-largest economy while we are negotiating with Turkey over its EU membership. And if it's no, then it's a real no.' (http://www.itv.com/news/2016-09-27/ nicolas-sarkozy-to-give-britain-chance-to-reverse-brexit-vote-if-elected- french-president/)

What about the economy?

The European Free Trade Association does actually have its own court.

Switzerland does not have access to the court, however, because it is not signed up to the EEA agreement.

Economic events could make the single market options more attractive to Downing Street.

If the political weather changed sufficiently Britain could even change its mind and decide to stay in the EU. There is legal uncertainty over whether a state can stop and reverse Article 50 once it is started, but it is unlikely that the rest of the EU would do anything to block such a move.

The Norwegians, who act as informal leaders of the group, may object.
Norway's European affairs minister, Elisabeth Vik Aspaker, articulated her concerns about Britain joining EFTA to the *Aftenposten* newspaper: 'It's not certain that it would be a good idea to let a big country into this organisation. It would shift the balance, which is not necessarily in Norway's interests.' (https://www.theguardian.com/world/2016/aug/09/norway-may-block-uk-return-to-european-free-trade-association)

The three European Supervisory Agencies on banking, insurance and security markets are not incorporated into the agreement.
The City law firm Slaughter and May warned that the absence of the European Supervisory Agencies 'may leave the UK financial services sector isolated.' (https://www.slaughterandmay.com/media/2535258/brexit-essentials-alternatives-to-eu-membership.pdf)

Only 8% of genuinely EU-originated law arrives in Norway.
The calculation that when you strip out international standards adopted by Brussels only 8% of genuinely EU-originated law makes it to Norway comes from the 'Stuck in the Middle with EU' report by the Adam Smith Institute. (http://www.adamsmith.org/stuck-in-the-middle-with-eu/)

Most of the work on a 'market solution' to Brexit, which would gradually disentangle the UK while keeping it in the single market, has been done by Dr Richard North under the name 'Flexcit' (Flexible Exit and Continuous Development) (http://www.eureferendum.com/themarketsolution.pdf)

The majority of the 'EU law' accepted by Norway actually originates in international standards that have been cut and pasted by the European Union into its own rules.
The comment that Brussels merely 'rubber stamps' regulations from global bodies is perhaps a little unfair. Supporters of the EU would say that it offers a democratic forum where these standards and requirements are debated and scrutinised.

It did this once before, over the Postal Services Directive.
Even though Norway has implemented 627 EU laws and only used the right of reservation once, the EU still applied pressure on it to change its mind and eventually it lifted the reservation. (https://fullfact.org/europe/eu-facts-behind-claims-norway/)

Norway has to pay in significantly less money than a full EU member.
A House of Commons library research paper found Norway's contribution to the EU in 2011 was £106 per capita, compared with the UK's net contribution of £128 per capita. (http://researchbriefings.parliament.uk/ResearchBriefing/Summary/RP13-42#fullreport)

But the Institute for Fiscal Studies concluded the cut would be more significant. 'If the UK were to make proportionally the same net contributions that Norway makes, for instance, these might amount to about half our current net contribution, leaving us with a strengthening of the public finances of around £4 billion.' (https://www.ifs.org.uk/uploads/publications/comms/r116.pdf)

It has the economic benefits of the single market but only has to implement 21% of all EU law.
The 21% figure for the amount of EU law that Norway must introduce is calculated by subtracting the EEA acquis (a body of rules) from the total number of EU laws in force. (http://eureferendum.com/blogview.aspx?blogno=85798)

Biscuits come under the designation of 'composite agrigoods'.
For the full horror of the EU's biscuit tariffs read (https://tradebetablog.wordpress.com/2016/08/18/eu-tariff-biscuit-annex1/)

That means a return to limits on how many bottles of spirits and packs of cigarettes can be brought back to the UK.
Current allowances of 800 cigarettes, 110 litres of beer, 90 litres of wine, 10 litres of spirits and 20 litres of sherry or port are likely to be downgraded to the limits imposed on those outside the EU, which stand at 16 litres of beer, four of wine and one of spirits. (http://www.telegraph.co.uk/travel/news/how-a-brexit-would-kill-off-the-booze-cruise/)

The EU has special rules for oranges, for example.
For more on the special rules on oranges, see (https://tradebetablog.wordpress.com/2016/09/10/oranges-litmus-test/)

Take the British sugar company Tate & Lyle.
For more on the long-running Tate & Lyle saga read (http://www.telegraph.co.uk/news/worldnews/europe/eu/9904266/The-EUs-sugar-ruling-thats-lefta-bitter-taste-at-Tate-and-Lyle.html)

Take chicken.

For more details on EU and UK poultry imports see (http://ec.europa.eu/agriculture/poultry/index_en.htm) And the Poultry Pocketbook 2015 (http://pork.ahdb.org.uk/media/73792/poultry-pocketbook-2015.pdf)

Similar changes could affect specialist producers.

There is a database of geographical indications for the EU, which makes for strangely compelling reading once you get into the detail of how various regions make their product. The rules on parmesan, for instance, demand that at least 75% of the dry matter of the fodder fed to the cow is produced within the geographical area. The database is here (http://ec.europa.eu/agriculture/quality/door/list.html;jsessionid=pL0hLqqLXhNmFQ_yFl1b24mY3t9dJQPflg3xbL2YphGT4k6zdWn34%21-370879141)

And the requirements for parmesan are here (http://eur-lex.europa.eu/LexUriServ/LexUriServ.do?uri=OJ:C:2009:087:0014:0019:EN:PDF)

How can we keep the UK together?

Guy Verhofstadt soon started making promising noises about Scottish membership.
Verhofstadt said: 'If Scotland decides to leave the UK, to be an independent state, and they decide to be part of the EU, I think there is no big obstacle to do that.' Such warmer messages are quite distinct from the EU's usual wariness on Scotland, not least because of the message it sends out to other separatist movements in Europe, particularly Spain. (http://www.dailyrecord.co.uk/news/politics/eus-chief-brexit-negotiator-agrees-8796253)

Westminster helps plug the gap in Scotland's £15 billion annual deficit.
As former prime minister Gordon Brown has pointed out, exports to rest of the UK are worth £48.5 billion to Scotland, compared with £11.6 billion to EU. A quarter of a million Scottish jobs are linked to the European single market, compared to one million linked to the UK one. (www.telegraph.co.uk/news/2016/06/29/gordon-brown-tells-scots-uks-single-market-worth-far-more-than-e/)

Around half a million SNP voters also voted to get out the EU.
This number is reached by taking the 36% of SNP voters who said they backed Brexit in Lord Ashcroft's research and applying it to the size of the SNP vote in the 2015 general election. (http://lordashcroftpolls.com/2016/06/how-the-united-kingdom-voted-and-why/)

What are we going to do?

Japan, for instance, has 1,000 business in the UK employing around 140,000 people.

A remarkably blunt letter from Japan to the UK following the Brexit vote urged it in no uncertain terms to stay in the single market. It read: 'A considerable number of Japanese businesses operating in Europe are concentrated in the UK. We have been informed of a variety of requests that these businesses have in relation to Brexit including: maintenance of trade in goods with no burdens of customs duties and procedures; unfettered investment; maintenance of an environment in which services and financial transactions across Europe can be provided and carried out smoothly; access to workforces with the necessary skills; and harmonised regulations and standards between the UK and the EU. The Government of Japan trusts that the UK and the EU, by heeding such requests to the fullest extent and responding to them in a cooperative manner, will maintain the current business environment or alleviate the impacts of any radical changes, so as to remain an attractive destination for doing business.' (http://www.mofa. go.jp/files/000185466.pdf)

He told the House of Commons Foreign Affairs Select Committee that Europe would fare worse than the UK if Article 50 ended without a deal and Britain fell onto WTO rules.

David Davis was asked by Conservative MP John Baron: 'If the Commission is going to try to square the circle, and a lot of elected politicians are worried about the ideological approach adopted by the Commission, it may actually encourage the Commission to push the timetable out and not bring it forward. Without getting into the minutiae of negotiations and red lines, have you formed a view on that?'

Davis replied: 'I don't think it can very easily. There are people who argue that article 50 disfavours somebody trying to leave. I don't agree with that, because that is only true if you fear the endgame. In fact, it puts a discipline on everybody, but everybody does understand that this process is quite quick by trade negotiation standards. We have some advantages in terms of existing commonality of standards and so on, but it is moderately quick, so they know they do not have time to waste. The endgame you described earlier—the sort of WTO endgame that the Chairman asked about—is not helpful for them by comparison with us. So it is not necessarily wise—there are other, bigger problems in timetables than that, so I don't think that is a big one.'

The transcript is here: (http://data.parliament.uk/writtenevidence/
committeeevidence.svc/evidencedocument/foreign-affairs-committee/impli-
cations-of-leaving-the-eu-for-the-uks-role-in-the-world/oral/38141.html)

More of the other 27 member states' goods are exported to the UK (16.9%) than to,
say, the US (16.5%). The UK buys £69 billion more in goods and services from the
EU than it sells to its countries. Across the EU, 5.8 million jobs are associated with
Britain, including 1.3 million in Germany and 500,000 in France.
For more information on these stats see these releases from the
European Commission (http://exporthelp.europa.eu/thdapp/display.
htm?page=st%2fst_Statistics.html&docType=main&languageId=en)

The House of Commons library (http://researchbriefings.parliament.uk/
ResearchBriefing/Summary/CBP-7213#fullreport)

And the Civitas think tank (http://www.civitas.org.uk/reports_articles/
uk-eu-trade-and-jobs-linked-to-exports/)

Germany exports about a fifth of all its new cars – 820,000 last year – to the UK.
German car exports to the UK are worth nearly €18 billion (www. ft.com/
content/f6cda050-20bb-11e5-aa5a-398b2169cf79)

Cyprus's incentives in the trade deal will be considerably smaller than Germany's.
For a full list of import/exports by EU states see (http://www.thisismoney.
co.uk/money/comment/article-3666465/How-does-EU-need-Britain-s-
trade-Brexit-means-ll-out.html)

Germany has the most to lose economically by hampering trade with Britain.
For a fuller breakdown of German exports see (http://www.tradingeconom-
ics. com/germany/exports)

The EU buys just under half of our total exports.
For a useful breakdown of UK-EU trade see (https://fullfact.org/europe/
uk-eu-trade/)

Brits spent £39 billion on holidays or business travel abroad in 2015.
For more on British family spending on holidays see (https://www.ons.
gov.uk/peoplepopulationandcommunity/leisureandtourism/articles/
traveltrends/2015#uk-residents-visits-abroad) and (http://www.ons.gov.
uk/peoplepopulationandcommunity/personalandhouseholdfinances/
incomeandwealth/compendium/familyspending/2015/chapter1overview)

Economists are now warily watching Britain's budget deficit, with some predicting it is set to increase by between £20 billion and £40 billion more than if we had stayed in the EU.

These figures are from the IFS' assessment of studies by the National Institute of Economic and Social Research (NIESR). (https://www.ifs.org.uk/uploads/publications/comms/r116.pdf)

Two hedge funds, Brevan Howard and Blue Crest, moved to Switzerland a few years ago and ran into problems.

The story of how traders beat a path back to London after getting richer – but also very bored – in Switzerland is like a morality tale about how money isn't everything. (https://www.ft.com/content/31681272-24b3-11e5-9c4e-a775d2b173ca)

The idea that the new directive is a good alternative to the current set-up is wrong.

For a good discussion of why the Markets in Financial Instruments Directive 2 will not be able to save City firms, see (https://medium.com/@dsquared-digest/the-third-country-equivalence-delusion-ebaa45757171#.k4py2t50r)

87% of the European staff working for the big five US investment banks staff in Europe are based in the UK.

This figure comes from a report by New Financial (http://newfinancial.eu/wp-content/uploads/2016/09/2016.09-What-do-EU-capital-markets-looklike-post-Brexit-a-report-by-New-Financial.pdf)

But after a few years economists will look at the cumulative data and find that Brexit cost the City nearly 10% of its capacity, 100,000 jobs and £12 billion in revenue.

These figures are again from PwC's pre-referendum report for TheCityUK (www.thecityuk.com/assets/2016/Reports-PDF/Leaving-the-EU-Implications-for-the-UK-FS-sector.pdf)

This has been well documented by the Bank of England, the Office of Budget Responsibility and the Institute of Fiscal Studies.

In October 2015, the Bank of England stated: 'Openness to labour flows – via migration – can allow an inflow of skills not otherwise available in the domestic economy. Ortega and Peri (2014) find that migration boosts long-run GDP per capita, acting both through increased diversity of skills and a greater degree of patenting. At the firm level, several studies further find that migration has a positive impact on productivity by diversifying the high-skilled labour employed by firms. And Miguélez & Moreno (2013) find that the mobility of researchers in Europe boosts patenting rates. A further range of studies find strong links between migration and trade, which may be explained by the fact that migrants can provide information that makes it easier for firms to start exporting to their home countries.' (http://www.bankofengland.co.uk/publications/Documents/speeches/2015/euboe211015.pdf)

In July 2013, a report by the Office of Budget Responsibility found: 'There is clear evidence that, since migrants tend to be more concentrated in the working-age group relatively to the rest of the population, immigration has a positive effect on the public sector's debt dynamics. This is shown in our sensitivity analysis, where higher levels of net inward migration are projected to reduce public sector net debt as a share of GDP over the long term relative to the levels it would otherwise reach.' (http://budgetresponsibility.org.uk/docs/dlm_uploads/2013- FSR_OBR_web.pdf)

In June 2016, IFS director Paul Johnson wrote: 'Immigration from the EU is good for the public finances. Young people in work contribute, on average, much more in taxes than they take out in benefits and public service spending. A large part of what government does is to take money from young workers and give it to pensioners. Without high net immigration the public finances would be in a worse state. If we were significantly to reduce the number of EU migrants, we would have to borrow more, raise taxes or spend less. (https://www.ifs.org.uk/publications/8317)

Those who arrived between 2001 and 2011 endowed the UK with productive human capital that would have cost it £6.8 billion in education spending.
From the UCL report: Positive economic impact of UK immigration from the European Union: new evidence (https://www.ucl.ac.uk/news/news-articles/1114/051114-economic-impact-EU-immigration)

Foreign students, who are disproportionately likely to be wealthy, well-educated and to start successful businesses, are particularly advantageous to have in the UK.
In 2011, the Department for Business Innovation and Skills found that international students put the total value of UK education and training exports to the economy at £14 billion in 2008/09. (https://www.gov.uk/government/publications/education-exports-estimating-their-value-to-the-uk)

Migrants go to countries where they think there are job opportunities and where they expect to be treated fairly.

For instance, immigration from Poland and other eastern European states fell following the financial crash. (http://siteresources.worldbank.org/EXTPREMNET/Resources/C17TDAT_297-320.pdf)

Brexiters, including Labour MPs, frequently argue that unskilled immigration depressed low and medium wages.

See the article by Leeds West Labour MP Rachel Reeves here (http://www.fabians.org.uk/wp-content/uploads/2016/09/FABJ4808_Europe_Report_130916_WEB_2.pdf)

Many studies find no downward effect on wages.

Research by London School of Economics found that 'areas of the UK with large increases in EU immigration did not suffer greater falls in the jobs and pay of UK-born workers' (http://cep.lse.ac.uk/pubs/download/brexit05.pdf)

The Bank of England, for instance, found that there might be a 1.8% drop in income for unskilled or semi-skilled workers.

Generally speaking, most studies have found a very modest reduction in unskilled wages where industries see migrants take jobs above a certain high threshold. Others have found wages in general have increased despite this slight drop. The Bank of England study is here (http://www.bankofengland.co.uk/research/Documents/workingpapers/2015/swp574.pdf)

A report from the Resolution Foundation after the referendum found that reducing immigration to the government's aim of around 100,000 would increase the wages of low-paid workers in the sectors most affected by between 0.2% and 0.6%.

The report on the impact of Brexit on wages is here (http://www.resolutionfoundation.org/media/press-releases/brexit-pay-squeeze-will-be-larger-than-boost-some-low-paid-workers-receive-from-lower-migration/)

There are enough Conservative opponents of a hard Brexit to defeat Theresa May.

Theresa May does have a couple of advantages in the Commons. Firstly, she can count on the support of the DUP. And secondly, the Labour leadership is not willing to campaign to stay in the single market because it objects to its state aid rules.

Britain needs to create a regulatory system across swathes of the country's policy agenda.

The full list of EU agencies which may need to be replicated in the UK is published here (http://www.allenovery.com/Brexit-Law/Documents/Macro/AO_GLIU_-_A_Brexit_Act_Aug_2016.pdf)

Some hard Brexiters suggest that the way to deal with this problem is to hand it to the courts.
Should you wish to read it, the Centre for Social Justice report suggesting that judges rules on regulatory standards is available here (http://www.centreforsocialjustice.org.uk/library/road-to-brexit)

The snapshot also only solves the problem of what happens to our domestic law.
For more detail on the difficult legal terrain Britain may be about to find itself, see (http://www.shlegal.com/news-insights/enforcing-judgments-after-brexit)

The Royal College of Veterinary Surgeons and the British Veterinary Association have warned that a sudden reduction in immigration would damage animal services in the UK.
The letter warning about veterinary services was all the more remarkable for coming from organisations who tend to stay away from day-to-day politics and concentrate on background policy work. It read: 'We have received reports that the increasing focus on foreign workers is causing personal distress to individual members of the veterinary profession who live and work in the UK. There are also reports of a negative impact on recruitment and retention: those involved in public health critical roles, such as meat hygiene, are having increasing difficulty recruiting much needed EU veterinary surgeons to work in the UK; leading experts from overseas are turning down employment offers from top UK universities; and many others are considering leaving the UK due to a feeling it is no longer welcoming to foreigners. There is a danger that the language and rhetoric around Brexit, alongside the ongoing uncertainty for non-British EU citizens, could seriously impact the veterinary profession's ability to fulfil its essential roles.' (https://www.bva.co.uk/news-campaigns-and-policy/newsroom/news-releases/veterinary-organisations-send-an-open-letter-to-pm-regarding-brexit-and-eu-vets/)

For years rural communities and eurosceptic MPs have complained that the EU interferes too much in farming.
An alternative would be just to ignore the EU as most farmers seem to do. In 2014 a study by the director general for internal policies found that

'all the available evidence points at persisting high rates of non-compliance in the large majority of member states in relation to the ban on routine tail-docking of pigs.' (http://www.europarl.europa.eu/RegData/etudes/STUD/2014/509997/IPOL_STU(2014)509997_EN.pdf)

38% of the UK's total production of sheep and lamb goes to the EU.
For more information on British farming's relationship with the EU see the National Farming Union's pre-referendum fact sheet (http://www.nfuonline.com/assets/61993)

Where leaving the EU will have a significant impact is on tariffs, which can be sky high on animal products.
Tariff rates for animal products are usually worked by a euro per 100 kg basis so can be hard to quantify. You can find those prices on the EU document. (http://eur-lex.europa.eu/legal-content/EN/TXT/HTML/?uri=OJ:L:2015:285:FULL&from=EN)
Cameron's team sourced its tariff calculations came from the Market Access Map resource (http://www.macmap.org/)

This will all take place under the supervision of a weakened and diminished government department.
Defra was hit by very significant budget cuts during austerity, with a 29% cut in 2010 and a projected 30% cut in 2015, although that may now not go ahead given the increased responsibilities it is about to take on. (http://www.bbc.co.uk/news/ uk-politics-11569160) (https://www.theguardian.com/environment/2015/nov/11/defra-hit-by-largest-budget-cuts-of-any-uk-government-department-analysis-shows)

If they end, some types of farming will decline.
For more details on farm subsidies and the types of farms which require them see (https://fullfact.org/economy/farming-subsidies-uk/)
Farms concerned with livestock like beef and sheep would be particularly vulnerable.
For more on the beef industry's reliance on subsidies: (http://beefandlamb.ahdb.org.uk/wp/wp-content/uploads/2013/05/p_cp_inthebalance.pdf)

In practical terms that means we control economic activity taking place up to 200 miles out to sea.
The 200 miles rule is part of the UN Law of the Sea Convention (http://www.un.org/depts/los/convention_agreements/texts/unclos/unclos_e.pdf#page=37)

This would not suit the British palate.
UK vessels land around 400,000 tonnes of fish each year in the UK, alongside up to 300,000 tonnes abroad. Britain remains a net importer of fish, however, with net imports of around 220,000 tonnes in 2014, worth £1.2bn. (http://researchbriefings.files.parliament.uk/documents/SN02788/SN02788.pdf)

This partly explains why the fishing industry was so stridently pro-Brexit during the campaign.
Some studies found as many as 92% of fishermen wanted out the EU, making them the most strongly eurosceptic section of British society (http://ukandeu.ac.uk/british-fishermen-want-out-of-the-eu-heres-why/)

Before the Council meets, the EU shares out the North Sea stocks with Norway.
For more on Norway's fishing arrangements see, which is also very good in general on Norway's approach to securing international influence (http://www. civitas.org.uk/content/files/TheNorwegianWay.pdf)

Now that it is leaving the EU, it will try to negotiate bigger fish quotas for UK fishermen.
For more details on the UK's fishing conundrum, see the House of Commons Library briefing paper 'Brexit: What next for UK fisheries?' (http://research-briefings.parliament.uk/ResearchBriefing/Summary/CBP-7669)

The evidence given to the House of Lords EU committee on fishing is also revealing (http://data.parliament.uk/writtenevidence/committeeevidence.svc/evidencedocument/eu-energy-and-environment-subcommittee/brexit-fisheries/oral/37841.html)

It is backed by The Financial Times, Chatham House, the Adam Smith Institute and countless others.
The Financial Times' Brexit briefing argued: 'The advantages of this are clear. By entering the EEA, the UK would formally leave the EU, thereby honouring the referendum decision. It would also protect access to the single market over the medium term, as British business desires. But once inside the EEA, the UK and EU would have plenty of time to try to agree a bespoke trade deal, something that cannot be concluded within the two-year Article 50 timeframe. Britain would also have far more time to strike trade deals with non-EU states, something that will take many years and which it cannot begin to do until it has formally left the EU.' (https://www.ft.com/content/931bffc8-5253-11e6-befd-2fc0c26b3c60)

Writing for Chatham House, Professor Richard G Whitman called an interim EEA deal 'a safe harbour in the brexit storm.' (https://www.chathamhouse.org/expert/comment/eea-safe-harbour-brexit-storm)

The Adam Smith Institute concluded: 'The least disruptive option now for the UK is to seek to agree a European Economic Area (EEA) relationship with the EU, prior to invoking Article 50. The EEA presents the best prospective short- and medium-term solution, providing Britain with a path away from full EU membership to a new status for a non-member that is tried and tested. It would also ease the UK's crushing political and diplomatic burden of simultaneously seeking to renegotiate its trade relationship with the EU and all its other trade partners.' (https://static1.squarespace.com/static/56eddde762cd9413e151ac92/t/5795e9137 25e254c7c8afa30/1469442330090/)

A parliamentary device likely to be used in the Great Repeal Bill to disentangle the vines of EU and UK law is the statutory instrument.
For more data on the increased use of statutory instruments see (http://www.legislation.gov.uk/uksi)
Campaigner and journalist Jane Fae has tracked the rise of statutory instruments (http://www.politics.co.uk/comment-analysis/2015/01/14/a-war-on-democracy-how-statutory-instruments-replaced-acts-o)

American pharma giants have an incredibly powerful and well-established lobbying operation.
For instance see the controversy over the Trans-Pacific Partnership's rules on intellectual property protections for biologics. (https:// www.ft.com/content/eb52ea88-cb46-11e5-be0b-b7ece4e953a0)

What it hates is NICE, the National Institute for Health and Care Excellence.
For more on how the US system of drug pricing acts to prevent almost any control on pharmaceutical companies' profits see (http://www.theatlantic.com/ health/archive/2014/05/why-medicine-is-cheaper-in-germany/371418/)

American tech firms are increasingly outraged by the EU's data protection rules.
The full text of the EU measures, which are extraordinarily wide-ranging, can be found here (http://statewatch.org/news/2015/dec/eu-council-dp-reg-draftfinal-compromise-15039-15.pdf)

Take REACH, the European regulation on the Registration, Evaluation, Authorisation & Restriction of Chemicals.

For instance compare the US Toxic Substances Control Act of 1976 with the EU's Reach regulation (https://www.epa.gov/laws-regulations/summary-toxic-substances-control-act)

This article provides a useful summary of the differences between the two chemical regulatory systems (https://echa.europa.eu/regulations/reach)

The People and Politics of the Badger Cull

'GRIPPING'
PATRICK BARKHAM
THE GUARDIAN

Badgered to Death

DOMINIC DYER
Foreword CHRIS PACKHAM

■ Why is the UK government killing thousands
of badgers against the advice of scientists?

BADGERED TO DEATH
The People and Politics of the Badger Cull
Dominic Dyer.
Foreword by Chris Packham
240 pages, Paperback (£8.99)
ISBN: 9780993040757
www.canburypress.com

The author

Ian Dunt is editor of Politics.co.uk and political editor of the *Erotic Review*. He also writes for a variety of newspapers and magazines, including *The Guardian* and *The Times*. He works in the press gallery in Parliament.

Ian is a regular contributor to news programmes on TV and Radio, including Newsnight, the Today programme, Sky News, Radio 5 and the Jeremy Vine show.

He specialises in European politics, immigration and asylum, free speech and civil liberties.